DOCTOR
INCORPORATED

Stop the Insanity of Traditional Employment
and Preserve Your Professional Autonomy

TOD STILLSON, MD

www.doctororincorporated.com

simpliMD.com

© SimpliMD All Rights Reserved

© Dr. Inc. All Rights Reserved

Disclaimer:

I am a family physician, author, blogger, and podcaster. I am not a lawyer, accountant, or financial planner. The information in this book should not be construed as personalized financial advice and is meant for general education and entertainment purposes.

COPYRIGHT © 2023 TOD A STILLSON, MD

All rights reserved.

DOCTOR INCORPORATED
Stop the Insanity of Traditional Employment and Preserve Your Professional Autonomy

ISBN 978-1-5445-3904-1 *Hardcover*
      978-1-5445-3905-8 *Paperback*
      978-1-5445-3906-5 *Ebook*

DOCTOR
INCORPORATED

To my dear wife, who fills me with joy and confidence as she encourages me to share with others my love for the medical profession.

CONTENTS

Foreword ix

Introduction xiii

1. You Are a Small Business 1

2. The Big Picture 19

3. You Have Earned Assets 51

4. Big Corporations Want Your Business Power, and So Should You 81

5. Rethinking Employment 95

6. Corrective Action 117

7. One Simple Change 137

8. What's Old Is New 159

9. How a PC Can Help You 181

10. The Gatekeepers 207

11. How to Form Your PC 223

12. You Need Your Own Team 239

Conclusion 257

Acknowledgments 263

About the Author 265

FOREWORD

Clink, clink, clink.

Clink, clink, clink.

Clink, clink, clink.

MY COINS WERE SLOWLY DROPPED INTO THEIR NEW HOMES in my jars labeled *give*, *save*, and *spend*. Based on my predetermined plan, I always put 10 percent in *give*, 50 percent in *save*, and 40 percent in *spend*. I had spent the whole afternoon picking up rocks in the yard to earn a few dollars from my parents, so it was nice to see the fruits of my labor slowly accumulate.

My name is John Stillson, and Dr. Inc. is my dad. I am currently starting my first year in family practice residency. Despite the intensive education we receive during our medical training, the presence of adequate financial education is sorely lacking. Most medical professionals and students have never learned the fundamental—yet critical—financial skills I absorbed as a child. If physicians are fortunate enough to have learned these skills, they often don't know how to apply them to their medical practice. If you identify with this, you should not feel guilty, because the problem is that *you don't know what you don't know*. There are significant financial forces at work that benefit from your financial and business illiteracy. They don't want you to *know what you don't know*.

This book examines the life of a doctor from the perspective of someone who has ridden the roller coaster of medicine up, down, and back up again. It lays the doctor's life out on the dissection table and takes it apart piece by piece, thus allowing you to see its inner workings, failures, and opportunities for optimization. Most attending physicians and residents don't know that they have options out there beyond the standard employment contract or fully winging it in private practice. If they do know this, they often don't have the time or energy to pursue it.

Medical students and residents, on the other hand, often ignore the importance of becoming literate in the financial workings of healthcare and plan to "cross that bridge when they get there," as they gasp for breath under mountains of student loan debt. What they don't realize is the power that comes with having early knowledge of the options that will be available to them when they start practicing as an attending physician. The lifetime financial impact after the application of this knowledge can be astounding.

Not everyone has to pick up rocks in the yard as their on-ramp to financial literacy, but everyone needs to have an on-ramp at some point. So let this book be your on-ramp. Ignorance is no longer an option.

John Stillson

July 2022

INTRODUCTION

I AM LIVING MY BEST LIFE. UNPLUGGED FROM MY JOB, CHILLED out with my family along a spectacular beach in Kauai, working on this book during a business trip covered by my company.

Ten years ago, this would have never happened because it was a world I never knew existed for doctors.

This book is written from the perspective of what I would tell my younger self about how to experience my best life as a physician. It is filled with personal and professional tips that would have saved me time, energy, and money had I been equipped with it thirty years ago when I earned my medical degree.

The information I am sharing with you would have spared me years of blindly following the same career path as my peers—a path that unknowingly eroded my personal and professional well-being each year that I was traditionally employed.

I accepted the tensions created by employment as typical for a young doctor and reacted to combat those pressures with personal resiliency measures and working harder. I naively thought this was my only option, as I was not aware of any other alternatives that would provide me relief. I reasoned the system I was employed within was unchangeable. Therefore, the changes had to occur from within me. I was both right and wrong, as I will explain later.

I am sharing my story with you because I want you to know I am one of you. I especially understand the various good and bad aspects of the employed doctor's life. I know how important it is to feel valued by your employer, receive fair compensation, and be empowered with professional autonomy. Despite its challenges, I believe employment is still an excellent option for most. However, the status quo system of traditional employment is not healthy for doctors and needs to be reshaped.[1]

I hope that I can help you avoid replicating one of the bigger mistakes that I made: passively trusting my employer to guide my professional life. This professional passivity is the default mode for most employed doctors who blindly place all their eggs in their employer's basket and then trust in the beneficence of their employer to support their professional development and well-being. Spoiler alert: it turns out you are a commoditized cog in their business machinery, and your personal and professional development is generally not their concern.[2] They love you for what you do for them, not for who you are.

---

[1] Simon G. Talbot and Wendy Dean, "Autonomy, Mastery, Respect, and Fulfillment Are Key to Avoiding Moral Injury in Physicians," TheBMJOpinion (blog), January 16, 2020, https://blogs.bmj.com/bmj/2020/01/16/autonomy-mastery-respect-fulfillment-key-avoiding-moral-injury-physicians/.

[2] Danielle Ofri, "The Business of Health Care Depends on Exploiting Doctors and Nurses," New York Times, June 8, 2019, https://www.nytimes.com/2019/06/08/opinion/sunday/hospitals-doctors-nurses-burnout.html.

Choosing the path of passive professional codependence within traditional employment leads to a gradual loss of control over your life. This loss of control is one of the underlying factors causing burnout for many in our profession.[3] In addition, the corporate takeover of the healthcare economy has resulted in doctors losing their small business powers and, thus, feeling trapped and morally injured by the soulless system of big business.[4]

My journey to near burnout within traditional employment, which was followed by my revival through the formation of my small business PC and its associated "employment lite" structure, has inspired me to want to share my discoveries with you.[5] I believe they will illuminate a hidden path that many of you can benefit from.

Ultimately, I want you to avoid the same slow fade of vitality that I experienced in my first fifteen years as a traditional employee. Due to the personal and professional crisis created by my professional passivity, I learned that I had to proactively manage my job structure and shape it to support my well-being. You will find out that your employer will not do this for you. Instead, it's up to you to do it for yourself.

I recognized that my path to thriving as a doctor had to include elements that restored my autonomy and actively prevented

---

[3] L. Allen Dobson Jr., "We Must Address the Causes of Burnout," *Medical Economics*, September 3, 2021, https://www.medicaleconomics.com/view/we-must-address-the-causes-of-burnout.

[4] Simon G. Talbot and Wendy Dean, "Physicians Aren't 'Burning Out.' They're Suffering from Moral Injury," *STAT*, July 26, 2018, https://www.statnews.com/2018/07/26/physicians-not-burning-out-they-are-suffering-moral-injury/.

[5] Craig Hunter and Neil Baum, "Physician-Hospital Alignment: 'Employment Lite,'" *The Journal of Medical Practice Management: MPM* 28, no. 4 (January/February 2013): 260–263, https://pubmed.ncbi.nlm.nih.gov/23547505/.

burnout.[6] Ultimately, the most significant changes that allowed me to adapt to the system of employment and still flourish as an individual included the following actions:

1. **Starting** my professional corporation (PC)

2. **Changing** my mindset

3. **Choosing** personal resiliency measures that helped my well-being

START YOUR PC

A fundamental component of preserving your autonomy—and the best place to **start**—is activating your unique power to incorporate yourself. Your professional corporation will act as a virtual entity that will allow you to control the professional assets that you have acquired at the launch of your medical career. Your PC will provide the necessary infrastructure for your professional life to be built upon much like land is needed to build a house. The parcel is more important than you probably realize, but it is typically an unassuming but critical component of the property. Your PC will support the evolution of your professional life much like land will support the dynamic changes of a house during the approximately three-decade span of your active medical career.

When you choose not to start your PC at the beginning of your career, you will be building your professional life on metaphorical land owned by others, most commonly your employer. This arrangement will result in an unhealthy codependency on them

---

6 Sarah Sloat, "Burned Out? Here's How You Can Recover, According to Experts," *Inverse*, April 17, 2022, https://www.inverse.com/mind-body/recover-from-burnout.

that will entrench their control of you, and make separating more difficult as time goes on. Although leasing space from them for your professional life is not always bad, ownership of that space through your PC is far better. It keeps you more in control of your professional life, which has important implications for your personal life as I will illuminate later.

I know prioritizing the formation of a professional corporation seems like an odd recommendation within a medical system that is voraciously eliminating private practice PCs from the marketplace.[7] This trend is precisely the reason that most of you likely have not even considered the idea of starting a PC. You recognize a private practice PC can rarely compete successfully against the deep pockets of their sizeable corporate opposition.[8] However, you likely have not considered the evolution of the modern PC into one that is no longer connected to a retail space or physical location.[9] Instead, it is a micro corporation that is built around your professional services and medical brain. This version is not a true competitor or threat to large corporations.

The new micro-PC is a ubiquitous virtual structure that is uniquely Dr. You, PC. This modern version of a PC will help you flourish throughout your career. Due to your individualized specialty training, professional interests, and personal style, no PC will be the same as yours. This makes you a one-of-a-kind

---

7   Praveen Suthrum, "Physician Practice Consolidation: It's Only Just Begun," *STAT*, February 27, 2020, https://www.statnews.com/2020/02/27/physician-practice-consolidation-its-only-just-begun/.

8   Len Strazewski, "8 Threats Facing Physician Private Practices," *AMA* (blog), American Medical Association, February 21, 2022, https://www.ama-assn.org/practice-management/private-practices/8-threats-facing-physician-private-practices.

9   Cecily Harris, "Guide to the Corporate Practice of Medicine for Virtual Care Companies," *Wheel* (blog), December 2, 2020, https://www.wheel.com/companies-blog/guide-to-the-corporate-practice-of-medicine-for-virtual-care-companies.

business. You have invested in yourself, created a unique style and identity, and earned the extraordinary power to cloak yourself in this highly individualized professional business structure.

Small business ownership has multiple other benefits, including supporting your well-being and enhancing your financial health. Overall, the earlier you can start your PC, the better. It will serve as a firm foundation for building your thriving career. So, you would be foolish not to activate your own individualized and virtual PC for your present and future benefit.

Employment does not obviate the benefits of forming a PC. This is a myth and one that needs to be dismantled. As I will demonstrate later in the book, the truth is that you can BOTH own and operate your PC while also being employed by a large corporation. Making you aware of your options, including the hidden PC-employment lite model, is one of the overarching purposes of this book.

I believe that PC-employment lite is your best choice for job structure because it will allow you to thrive holistically while also working within the relative safety of a large corporate employer's harbor. It still supports your employer's goal for physician alignment, but provides you with greater control over your professional life. It is a win-win business arrangement that addresses a foundational defect in the system of employment which is the loss of professional autonomy for doctors. This systemic flaw must change as a needed solution for the current burnout crisis. The PC-employment lite model combats burnout by enhancing your well-being through the preservation of your professional autonomy. Quite simply you are placed back in control of your professional life by activating one of your most important earned assets: your small business power to start your PC.

CHANGE YOUR MINDSET

The real challenge goes beyond helping you visualize this space of starting your PC or knowing that the PC-employment lite model even exists. Instead, it involves helping you overcome the mental hurdle that you have the ability, know-how, and time to run your micro-PC. Younger professionals tend to depend on their employers to direct their career development while also expecting them to cover everything else related to practicing medicine in the modern marketplace. This typically means that you don't need to, nor want to, know how to run a business. Employment, by definition, allows you to outsource this work to someone else who manages it for you. For most doctors, the freedom to not be in charge of a medical business is one of the most appealing aspects of employment.

This mindset informs and reinforces your acceptance of your business illiteracy and your choice to allow your employer to manage the business of medicine. Even if you wanted to start your PC, this acknowledged business deficit causes you to fear that you don't have the skills or time needed to run a business.[10]

Thus, you relegate starting a professional corporation to those who are natural entrepreneurs or have an MBA. That is because you envision an older version of a PC that includes running a retail medical business, managing employees, populating business spreadsheets, spending a lot of time overseeing it, and competing in the marketplace. Although this version is an option, it is not what I am proposing.

---

10 Evgenia Galinskaya, "7 Reasons Why Some Doctors Will Never Start a Business," *Pulse* (blog), LinkedIn, December 13, 2014, https://www.linkedin.com/pulse/7-reasons-why-some-doctors-evgenia/.

I am proposing you start the modern, slimmed-down, more-refined micro-version of a PC for your use in association with your professional services. This individualized small business is very lean and relatively easy to operate. It can be used in almost any job structure, and the business operations of it can be efficiently outsourced so that you are not bogged down with having to manage it.

But in order to move in this direction, you must shift your mindset in three ways. The first is you must understand that starting your micro-PC does not mean you are going into private practice, rather it means you are preserving and protecting your professional business power. The second is that choosing employment does not mean you won't benefit from a PC, because the truth is that you can use a PC within virtually any employment structure. The third is that starting a PC will not result in you missing out on the freedom to not operate a medical business, because the micro-PC has a simplicity that makes outsourcing its management quite easy.

CHOOSE A NEW PATH

One of the aspects of PC-employment lite that I discovered was most important to me was the way it restored and preserved my professional autonomy. Regaining my autonomy turned out to incredibly improve my well-being. The lesson learned for me was that choosing a professional path that preserves my autonomy is fundamental to my well-being as a doctor. In most cases, traditional large corporate employment will erode your autonomy, and thus my admonition to you is to choose a different path. But you can't passively trust employers to provide you with a table of options, as they are not obligated to do this. Instead, you will have to proactively request it yourself. It's kind of like choosing something on the "hidden menu" at a restaurant. The option is there, but you have to know it and bring it up; otherwise you will be funneled to choose from the same menu as the masses. In the employed doctor world, that means you will have to propose a job structure that is on their invisible menu. It turns out this is the same structure that employers use to onboard private practice doctors into their safe harbor. It's available, but not visible, so you just have to know to ask for the PC-employment lite option. But, like most doctors who represent themselves at the contract negotiation table, you just don't know what you don't know, so you miss it.

I hope that as you read this book, you are inspired to believe that you can and should form a modern PC that can be used in conjunction with employment, and you need not relegate the concept of a PC solely to the space of private practice.

I love my life as a doctor, and I want you to love yours as well. I believe sharing my experiences and discoveries with you about PCs and the employment lite model will help you arrive at your best life.

This book will add me to the growing group of doctors providing innovative answers to the physician burnout crisis. There are ample resources available on personal and professional resiliency solutions for you. Thus, this will not be my focus in these pages. However, I strongly suggest you **choose** to equip yourself with these mindfulness skills because they are essential to the well-being of every doctor.

I aim to provide you with a novel solution to the broken system of employed physicians. This solution will lead you to **start** something new in the form of your individual micro-PC that will serve as the foundation to help you live your best life. I also want to inspire and inform you that there are options beyond traditional employment. By combining these two ideas, you can use your PC to **change** the current status quo of employment, which is often detrimental to your well-being.

One of my favorite authors is Mark Batterson. He inspires me to go after the big goals that can feel impossible to accomplish. In his book, *Win the Day,* I like how he encourages each of us in the process of reaching for something better:

> *"If you want to change your life, start by changing your story."*[11]

At the turning point of my story, I knew change was needed personally and professionally, so I decided to seize control of the narrative and actively shape it to my benefit. I visualized my best future, chose the right path to get me there, and created the proper infrastructure to support that journey.

Let the ideas of this book inspire you to proactively do the same by using all of your earned professional assets to map out a future that supports your well-being and allows you to thrive. In particular, I think you will love the benefits of using your modern PC as a mile marker to this path.

Employment need not be an obstacle to doing this, nor should your fear of running a small business be one. As you will see, I have successfully overcome both of these, and I know you can too.

---

[11] Mark Batterson, *Win the Day: 7 Daily Habits to Help You Stress Less & Accomplish More* (Colorado Springs: Multnomah, 2020), 8.

You got this!

Before you dive in, let's do a quick summary of the book chapters so that you can know where we are going with things.

IN THE BEGINNING—YOUR PROFESSIONAL POWERS

Chapter 1: Discover the historical basis and modern reasons why you are a small business professional and how that power can help you thrive by preserving your autonomy.

Chapter 2: Your life as a doctor can be divided into three stages, and this book primarily focuses on the very dynamic Stage 2, which is your attending physician phase. Stage 2 is best built on the foundation of your PC, rather than a space fully controlled by your employer.

Chapter 3: Take inventory of all the assets you have earned at each professional stage and use each to live your best life. Activating your small business powers early in your career, rather than completely subjugating them to your employer, will help you thrive.

THE PROBLEM OF CORPORATIZATION

Chapter 4: Corporate employers are most interested in your professional business powers and how they can economically benefit from them and are less interested in your professional vitality.

Chapter 5: Employment is a great option for most doctors, but systemic adaptations are needed to help reduce your risk of burnout as an employee.

THE SYSTEMIC SOLUTION—PRESERVING YOUR PROFESSIONAL AUTONOMY

Chapter 6: PC-employment lite is a systemic correction to physician employment that can increase your professional autonomy and improve your household financial position.

Chapter 7: Converting to a PC-employment lite structure is a simple but profound change that allows your employer to have the alignment they want while providing you with personal and professional benefits (autonomy).

Chapter 8: Much like doctors of yesteryear, forming your PC at the beginning of your career is an essential component to preserving and leveraging this professional asset. It can then be used within a large number of professional job structures and integrated into a business enterprise model.

Chapter 9: Your individual PC will unlock the many financial benefits afforded to small business owners throughout our country.

Chapter 10: You will encounter resistance to rethinking how you can use a modern PC in the marketplace, and the first hurdle you must overcome is yourself.

Chapter 11: You must know the essential steps to start and maintain your small business PC.

Chapter 12: You will benefit from forming a business team that supports your PC as well as your personal and professional interests.

Conclusion: Start your PC now—it is the most critical step to avoid burnout and flourish as a doctor.

Tod Stillson MD
Aka

CHAPTER 1

YOU ARE A SMALL BUSINESS

Just a few years ago, a doctor did not have to be reminded of the notion that they were a business. It was built into their mindset. The assumption was that one would enter the marketplace after completing training and set up or join a small company known as a private practice. A physician was, by default, a small business person.

The professional and personal autonomy that is built into operating a small healthcare business is nicely aligned with the DNA of most doctors. We like being in charge and are trained to be analytical decision-makers with an aptitude for continually learning new things. These all overlap with the skillset needed to be a successful small business person. On top of that, the mental architecture of developing and executing a clinical plan with a patient shares some congruency with doing the same with a small business plan. The common denominator for the exam room and the business office is that you are in control and empowered to be a decision-maker.

HISTORICAL BASIS

Your economic power has been well documented over the centuries. Historically, physicians could earn income by teaching students or serving as public doctors. Ancient Greece and Rome had examples of healthcare institutions that both provided payment for physicians and guaranteed treatment for the community. The Greek and then Roman civilizations often supported physicians within municipalities and framed their service as a public duty and calling.

In particular, the Greek physician Hippocrates, who is often called the "father of medicine," has influenced the ethical mindset of this long-standing tension between professionalism and business. The Hippocratic tradition, which is famous today due to the Hippocratic Oath, argued that the physician ought to prioritize treatment and not fees. Additionally, if a patient was suffering economic hardship, the physician ought to dispense with payment altogether. This was summarized in his influential writings such as the following example:

"Consider carefully your patient's superabundance or means. Sometimes give your services for nothing, calling to mind a previous benefaction or present satisfaction. And if there be an opportunity of serving one who is a stranger in financial straits, give full assistance to all such. For where there is love of man, there is also love of the art."[12]

His philosophy of how to blend medical business and the ethical duty to equally help the public has served as a cornerstone mindset for physicians throughout the thousands of years that followed.

In both ancient and modern times, Western Civilization doctors have had a long-standing tension regarding their professional obligations to serve versus running a business. For example, English physicians could not legally bill for their services hundreds of years ago. Instead, following the Roman practice, patients paid "honoraria" voluntarily in connection to medical care. This legal architecture supported the Hippocratic duty of physicians to provide care regardless of a patient's ability to pay.

THE US HISTORY

Ultimately, the progressive civic philosophy and legal rules that differentiated professions from businesses in Western Europe did not survive the trip to the American colonies. Instead, medical practitioners here were viewed through the eyes of business-law principles right from the beginning. They were allowed to charge and collect fees based on the services they provided and careful consideration for the person's ability to pay. Thus from

---

12 Hippocrates, *Hippocrates: Volume I: The Loeb Classical Library*, ed. T. E. Page, E. Capps, W. H. D. Rouse, A. Post, and E. H. Warmington, trans. W. H. S. Jones (London: William Heinemann Ltd, 1957), 319 reprinted in Internet Archive, accessed November 30, 2022, https://archive.org/details/hippocrates01hippuoft/page/318/mode/2up.

the onset, physicians in America did not fully follow the "public calling" principle and its associated honorarium system. Rather, they followed the small business practices of the newly formed American capitalist system, which prioritized private ownership over government or institutional control. As this book unfolds, this business principle that was baked into the American Revolution is an essential concept for us to return to.

When joined with the Hippocratic professional and ethical principles, it later morphed into the adoption of a subjectively driven "sliding scale" medical services price model that allowed doctors to charge what they perceived the patient could afford. The remuneration could include a mixture of goods, services, or money. This sliding scale matrix allowed for the fusion of a doctor's duty to serve the public equally with the preservation of one's interest in operating a business.

THE PRESENT

This historical journey affirms that a doctor's knowledge and expertise in providing medical services to patients has always had a built-in monetized value, which in the United States has long been viewed as a small private business. For years, the value of a doctor's services was self-determined and influenced by the free market forces that were interconnected to the location of the medical business.

This all changed with the introduction of private health insurance, primarily after WWII. This was further accelerated by the federal government's version of health insurance in 1965 when Medicare and Medicaid were signed into law. Their arrival signaled the loss of control of physicians subjectively choosing prices in conjunction with the free market defining the value of their services. As these parties were empowered, they began to control and determine the value of a physician's professional service.

As a result, in the present state, the value of your services is nearly entirely determined by third parties and not by you. Those third parties place worth on your work in two ways:

The first way involves how payors decide to pay you, or your employer, for the medical services rendered. In this loop, the third party will **reimburse** you or your employer for your work, rather than pay you for it at the time care is provided. Unlike payment which involves an agreed-upon business arrangement in which you get money at the point of service, reimbursement means you will get your full payment later.

In order to be paid, you have to prove that you have done the work; thus, this system of "proving" your work has led to the rise of the electronic health record (EHR). This digital platform is not so much a repository of health information as it is the business ledger for mining revenue. Your employer's EHR, a/k/a cash register, is based upon your translation of your medical care into numerical codes called current procedural terminology (CPT) and international classifications of diseases version 10 (ICD-10) designations. The complexity of this system has become a huge administrative burden for doctors, as it consumes a large portion of any patient encounter. It has wholly displaced the highly efficient small business practice of paying for your service or goods at the point of care, at a price that the parties agreed upon.

The second way the value of your professional work is translated is within the **compensation** loop between you and your employer. Here the value of your work is encoded into a standardized unit called a Work Relative Value Unit (wRVU). This represents a measurement that accounts for time, skill, training, and the intensity of the service you provided. Each CPT code is typically assigned a correlating wRVU value. This is all used by employers to determine your compensation via an agreed-upon productivity compensation matrix, or salary.

The wRVU system is meant to equally standardize the value of your services regardless of location and specialty. However, it gets even more complicated when the dollar value of each wRVU is further organized into fair market ranges by another layer of third parties (most commonly the medical group management association—MGMA for short). These groups make their private data purchasable to employers and doctors, but not to the public. This, in turn, often leads to what is called information asymmetry for individual doctors whose employers have access to this fair market compensation data, but the data is less accessible to individual doctors because it tends to be cost-prohibitive for you to personally access it. Thus they will authentically tell you that your compensation is at a fair market rate, but what they will fail to mention is that it is a range and not an actual number. Thus they can save money by choosing a lower range value for your wRVU compensation rather than an upper range value.

IT'S COMPLICATED

Given this highly complex business model that favors third-party control of the economic variables, it's no surprise that most of you will choose to trade in the business value of your professional knowledge to employers whose job is to extract revenue for your associated services. You likely reason that this trade will allow you to fulfill your altruistic desire to help people rather than run a business. Money can be a barrier to caring for patients, and many of us would simply prefer to focus on tending to the patient's medical needs and allow someone else to handle the business exchange. In many regards, offloading the financial interaction is a more altruistic version of medicine that harkens back to the Hippocratic professional call to serve the public, both rich and poor.

During my life, I have had the privilege of providing medical care to the impoverished and disadvantaged within the US and around the world. I have served in ongoing clinics as well as pop-up clinics in many remote villages and on numerous continents. Most of the time, there was no monetary barrier to entry for the patients, nor were documentation requirements associated with the care. Instead, there was just a patient needing care paired with my knowledge and expertise, one encounter at a time. In those moments, a deep sense of pleasure is derived because the care is stripped of the transactional barriers and colored by the purity of my desire to use my skills to help someone in need. That exhilarating and rewarding feeling always reminds me that this is why I chose medicine as my career. It feels good to help people without my care being continuously monetized.

Don't get me wrong, even if you share these good motives, most of us also deeply understand that our professional services indeed do have a value that is generally translated into a high income in the US system. You can expect to receive this pot of gold as you start your career, just as I did. This expectation is why you are willing to accept the high cost of the runway associated with the launch of your career as an attending physician. This runway is known as your medical training, and it truly represents your expensive investment in your future small business powers known as Dr. You.

COMMON PATH

Let's look at a typical doctor who has chosen the path of corporate employment.

Dr. Tony is happily employed as a physician for a hospital system that is located near his wife's family. It's his first job, and it provides him with a simple way to launch his career in medicine. With the sizable fair market value paychecks, the signing bonus, and the loan forgiveness program, he can now begin paying off debts, buy a house, and own a car that is less than five years old. As a new attending physician, he now has the time and resources to live his preferred lifestyle in a location with a good quality of life and some predictable time away from medicine. In addition, he and his wife are now empowered to grow their family, knowing they can finally afford it.

He celebrates his arrival in this attending physician space and expects a certain level of professional and personal autonomy that is afforded to most physicians. Professionally he begins to integrate his style, interests, and identity within his chosen specialty. This individuation process is very satisfying due to the self-actualization elements associated with it. He is emerging from his generic specialty title and genuinely becoming an individual whose knowledge, expertise, and style are unique to him. He embraces his high income and robust lifestyle from his job and feels satisfied leaving the hassles of the business of medicine to his employer.

Medical business seems complicated, risky, and time-consuming, so avoiding this in exchange for the simplicity of employment, particularly shift work employment, is a no-brainer. It's a great life, and finally being able to unlock his pent-up delayed gratification associated with training feels incredible!

MEETING YOUR NEEDS

Tony's story is a snapshot of the path that you—like many doctors—are apt to take in the early years of your professional career. That is because prospective employers are aware that you have some immediate needs that they are more than happy to meet to entice you to join them.

First on your mind is the need to erase your large and burdensome student loans that now can average a mind-boggling $300,000 or more per person.[13]

Secondly, you have chosen to accept your business and financial illiteracy as a result of your singular focus on your medical training. It's not that you don't care about these areas, but you just haven't had the time to explore them, nor were they built into medical education and professional training.

You intelligently react to these two pressure points by targeting employment positions that offer you a solution to these two menacing problems. Physician employers provide the needed answers with loan payback bonuses along with fair market value compensation packaged in a turnkey clinical job. This is especially appealing when compared to entering private practice with its associated high startup costs or expensive buy-in processes with partnerships or group practices. Beyond that, you note private practices are vanishing from the landscape, so you reason that it's not wise to join or start private practice when they appear to be losing ground in the marketplace.

---

13 Jennifer Calonia, "What's the Average Medical School Debt in 2022?," *Forbes*, May 13, 2022, https://www.forbes.com/advisor/student-loans/average-medical-school-debt/.

It's no surprise that this all adds up to driving 89 percent or more of graduating residents to choose the safe harbor of employment.[14] As a result, physician employees are now the majority job structure in the US, and this is growing annually.

However, there is a downside to this trend. Your employer now becomes your boss, usurps your identity, requires conformity to their standard operating procedures and policies, and ultimately exerts control over your schedule and professional services. As time goes on, the associated loss of power and autonomy within your professional life can lead to a tipping point of job dissatisfaction and even burnout.

YOU ARE A MEDICAL BUSINESS

Your professional services are valuable, and when they are informed by their historical roots in the US, they automatically make you a medical business. You alone get to determine whether to unlock this business power for yourself or trade in its power to your corporate employer to unlock. In today's world of medical employment, many physicians are unaware that they even possess this power as an earned asset.

Broadly speaking, you are part of a distinctive family of service professionals that exist in many different industries. These include lawyers, dentists, architects, accountants, financial advisers, and engineers, among others. Each one can offer customized, knowledge-based services to their clients within a business arrangement. Unlike other types of businesses, professional service firms sell knowledge and expertise—not visible,

---

14 Merritt Hawkins, *2021 Survey of Final-Year Medical Residents* (Dallas: Merritt Hawkins, 2021), 9, https://www.merritthawkins.com/trends-and-insights/article/surveys/2021-survey-of-final-year-medical-residents/.

physical products. Their products are generally intangible and are not amenable to economies of scale on the "cost of goods sold." But their services do have value, and this, in turn, generates revenue for their business.

You should let the past inform your future—by activating your individualized small business as a professional. This systemic directive was signaled as a foundational component to the vitality of the Republic by our founding fathers, whereby they emphasized the prioritization of private ownership over government or institutional control. This principle reflected their understanding that the well-being of the individuals within the Republic would be threatened if there was too much institutional control over their lives. This historical guardrail points toward a solution to the current burnout crisis associated with the corporatization of medicine. That solution is a return to doctors forming and using a professional corporation (PC) to preserve their professional autonomy.

You may think that a PC is unnecessary if you're not going into private practice. But before you move on, I invite you to learn why your assumptions about employment and PCs are wrong. I am going to share with you a personal discovery that I made a decade ago that busted this myth, and how adopting it into my professional life changed the course of my career. I wouldn't exactly call it a secret path, but I wouldn't say it's easily visible to most of you, either. So get ready to have your eyes opened.

BURNOUT PREVENTION AND PC-EMPLOYMENT LITE

The loss of professional autonomy that is experienced through the current state of medicine harms, injures, and impairs you on many levels.[15] Therefore, the restoration of your professional autonomy is a crucial ingredient to both preventing and recovering from burnout.[16] Physicians can much more resiliently autocorrect themselves under the pressures of corporate employment and thrive again, but first they must address the structural flaw of traditional employment's erosion of their professional autonomy.

I know from personal experience that when my professional and personal autonomy were fading within traditional employment, I was heading towards burnout. But my autonomy was reinvigorated through the formation of my PC-employment lite contract, also known as a Professional Services Agreement (PSA). As part of this arrangement, I was required to have my own business entity—my PC. My employer then contracted with my PC for my professional services, rather than to me individually. It was now transformed into a business-to-business relationship.

To be clear, this employment model is still a flavor of employment and not necessarily an escape from it. There are still aspects of professional life that I don't fully have control over, but the space created by the parallel operation of my PC has created freedom and power that is not found in traditional employment alone.

And this is why you need to place PC-employment lite on your radar. It represents a needed structural correction to the current

---

15 Simon G. Talbot and Wendy Dean, "Autonomy, Mastery, Respect, and Fulfillment Are Key to Avoiding Moral Injury in Physicians," *TheBMJOpinion* (blog), January 16, 2020, *https://blogs.bmj.com/bmj/2020/01/16/autonomy-mastery-respect-fulfillment-key-avoiding-moral-injury-physicians/*.

16 Pamela Hartzband and Jerome Groopman, "Physician Burnout, Interrupted," *The New England Journal of Medicine* 382, no. 26 (June 25, 2020): 2485–2487, https://doi.org/10.1056/NEJMp2003149.

state of employment that will go a long way towards helping you live your best life and avoid burnout. This is because it allows you to tap into the overarching benefits of small businesses and ultimately increases your professional autonomy.

Simultaneously it provides all the benefits of employment while addressing one of the fundamental flaws of physician employment, which is the loss of professional control. Your PC fills your autonomy tank, and corporate work empties it. Combining the two will help keep this crucial professional need balanced for you. This is a better version of employment than the traditional paradigm where your professional autonomy is constantly assaulted and your only recourse to fill your tank is personal resiliency methods.

THE NEW PC

As I wind up this chapter about your small business power, I believe it is critical to address an aspect of the changing PC-employment lite equation. Traditional PCs are slowly disappearing, and a modern version is now replacing them. The contemporary version is a micro version and doesn't compete with large corporations but instead collaborates with them individually.

Employers are more familiar with the private practice PC, which has historically been the home for most physicians. Thus the origins of the PC-employment lite model are tightly connected to this interface. With this in mind, when large companies recruit seasoned physicians, they come prepared to offer contracts that unite with these doctors and their PC framework. This older version of a PC typically included a medical office building, medical equipment, the small business itself—including employees, and of course, the professional services of the physician owner(s). Each of these elements has to be addressed contractually when a private practice doctor becomes an employee, and the purchase of their small business assets is typically hard-wired into the deal.

This is in contrast to new graduates or long-time employed mid-career physicians who come to employers without any business wrap-around. They are more easily contractually assimilated with their professional services. Rather than small business assets to be purchased, young doctors typically present to large corporations with personal liabilities (debt) that they hope will be bought by their employer as part of their recruitment deal.

Due to this dynamic, employers don't expect to interact with PCs for young doctors and physicians with a prior employment pedigree. In fact, employers often view a PC designation as a signal that you don't intend to be employed long-term, and thus they may express concern about hiring you through your PC. They fear not having total control of you and are also unfamiliar with the newer version of a micro-PC that doesn't necessarily compete with them.

Thus, when I talk about starting your PC, I am NOT talking about the older PC version that is tightly associated with private practice and independent medical care. Instead, I am talking about a modern micro-version that is more of a virtual corporation that houses your intangible and tangible professional assets. It allows you to parse out your professional services, knowledge, and expertise to an increasingly diverse healthcare economy that is not geographically locked in.

I am pointing you towards your power to create a PC that can be either located within or outside your employer's safe harbor. In either case, you can form a PC and use the same bridge as your former private practice peers to access the free market interests with your professional skills, services, expertise, or knowledge. This can include your primary employer but also can involve business interests outside your employer's domain. We are now part of a global economy that is not constrained by local physicality and therefore does not compete directly with your primary employer. Your own PC allows you to connect with people and organizations who value your knowledge and services anywhere in the world.

As an example, I recently spoke to a specialist who resides in Southern California, but 75 percent of her professional services are delivered to patients in the Midwest through the power of digital communication. Her PC has a PSA with her hospital in Southern California, and the contract has a regional non-compete. However, in the new world of medicine, this has left the door open for her to connect with others outside their reach who value her virtual expertise.

Her PC has made it easy for her to have two sources of professional income that are geographically separated by thousands of miles. By the way, you may ask why she just doesn't move to the Midwest where most of her work is done, and the answer is that lifestyle, quality of life, and family ties keep her anchored on the West Coast as her preferred home. In the end, her more nimble and virtual version of her PC is not tied down to a brick-and-mortar location where she must physically deliver her services. Instead, it opens the door to possibilities due to her PC's ubiquitous nature and its ability to divide out her professional services.

This reframing of a PC to a more modern virtual container that wraps around your professional assets is what I want you to have in mind when you consider incorporating yourself and then contemplate the PC-employment lite structure.

Peter Drucker is considered the founder of modern management theory and practice. His writings and philosophies have heavily influenced government and corporate business management concepts in the latter part of the twentieth century. I like how he elucidates the necessary component for systemic change when he says:

> "If you want something new, you have to stop doing something old."

This same idea was said differently by the genius scientist Albert Einstein, whose theory of relativity provided new understandings of how everything in the universe worked together systematically. He is famously credited for defining insanity through the eyes of a physicist when he said:

> "Insanity is doing the same thing over again, and expecting different results."

Too many of you know that doing the same thing as your peers by following the old path of traditional employment and believing you will somehow avoid being among the 50% who are burned out is the same irrational thinking that Einstein associated with insanity. This subtle form of insanity will unfortunately, statistically, happen to more than half of you unless you quit doing something old.

You are at risk of missing out on your best life unless you do something different than accepting what you are currently being offered through traditional employment.

Drucker and Einstein are both exactly right, and that is why I exhort you to stop the insanity of traditional employment and do something new to preserve your professional autonomy.

SUMMARY

- Historically doctors have operated as a small business that was fused with their altruistic call to serve everyone regardless of their ability to pay.

- Doctors are a unique group of professionals who are given the power to start a professional corporation (PC).

- Employment lite is a hidden employment model that allows you to use your PC while remaining employed.

- Starting your own professional corporation will provide you with more autonomy as a small business owner.

- The modern micro-PC is a virtual container for your professional assets and is different from the older private practice version of a PC.

- The path to avoiding burnout for doctors involves making a systemic change by stopping something old and doing something new.

CHAPTER 2

THE BIG PICTURE

I GREW UP IN A HOME THAT WAS GUIDED BY THE PROTESTANT work ethic. This old Calvinist doctrine of a livelihood serving as the source of one's value—and a sign of God's favor—was hardwired into me. I was taught to rise early, work hard at my obligations, collect a paycheck from my employer, and enjoy the satisfaction of doing this honestly while surrounded by the rich fabric of family and friends who did the same. This was the ethos of my working-class family, where I became the first to attend college.

Within this mindset, I embraced medicine as my calling and forged my identity around it. I am passionate about our profession, and I want you to enjoy it as much as I do. Over time I wisely came to separate my identity from my medical work, but I still have a deep appreciation for the many holistic benefits of being a doctor.

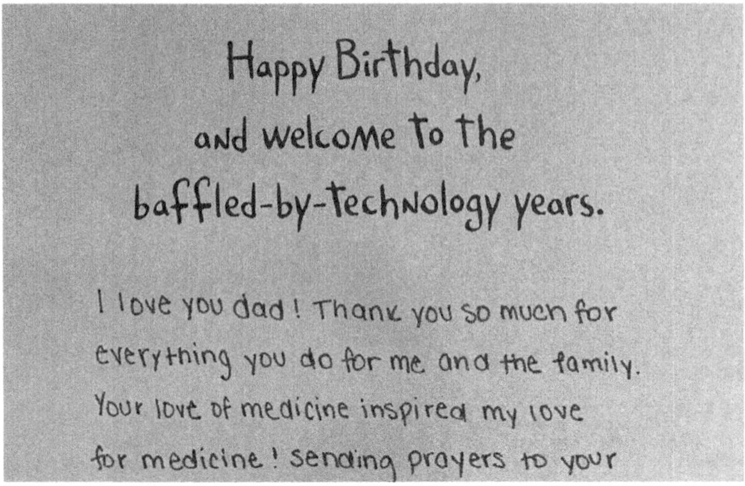

> Happy Birthday,
> and welcome to the
> baffled-by-technology years.
>
> I love you dad! Thank you so much for everything you do for me and the family. Your love of medicine inspired my love for medicine! Sending prayers to your

Figure 2.1

My family knows how much I love my medical life, and since imitation is the most sincere form of flattery, it's special to me that three of my five children are in the medical field. This inspiration was documented by my youngest daughter in a recent birthday card. (See Figure 2.1) My oldest, John, plans to be a family doctor like me and is just beginning his residency. Since I have endeavored to disciple, coach, and support each of my children in their life trajectories, his decision to follow in my footsteps led me to reflect on what truths would help him thrive as a medical professional.

I want to help him love his medical career as much as I love mine. In fact, I am hopeful that by vulnerably sharing my highs and lows, I can help him avoid some of my mistakes. There are also some trade secrets for employed doctors that I am confident can provide some helpful guardrails to him. I have thoroughly enjoyed coaching him up to this point, but I realize so much more lies ahead.

YOUNG DOCTOR MINDSET

Before you get too nostalgic, John does not plan to come back home and join my medical practice, and there are three primary reasons for this. First, his wife is from Alabama, and they will likely migrate to the South rather than the Midwest as they start their family. Second, I am an employed doctor, and although I own and operate my own professional corporation, John would have to choose employment with my large corporate employer and not with me. Thus, he would not be coming back to "take over the family business." Thirdly, John does not plan to make a long career out of medicine. Instead, he plans to use his high income to reach financial independence and then step away from medicine within ten years. In fact, he already has started his own crypto investment fund called Ascension Capital and serves as an agent for a small physician-centric agency that I own called SimpliMD.

Admittedly, he likely observed the benefits of both medical and non-medical small businesses from me and plans to do it better. On top of that, his wife's family has operated a highly successful small business for years, and she shares a similar desire to leverage her accounting degree into small business success, having already started a few side businesses.

My relationship with John provides me some insight into the mindset of Millennials (born 1981–1996) and Gen Zers (born 1997–2012), who are quickly becoming the next wave of doctors in our society.[17] I have also learned a lot through my new associate, who has joined me at my practice. Anthony and his wife

---

17 Joanne Finnegan, "3 Things to Know about Recruiting and Retaining Millennial Doctors," Fierce Healthcare, April 12, 2018, *https://www.fiercehealthcare.com/practices/recruiting-and-retaining-millennial-doctors-comphealth-lisa-grabl.*

have provided me with fresh perspectives on what's important to young medical professionals and their families.

Both John and Anthony have forced me, as a Gen-Xer (born 1965–1980) physician, to re-think many things about life and medicine. Like any good relationship, we co-learn from one another, and I am thankful for the mutuality in these friendships. The most significant thing I've learned from them is they believe medicine is just a job and not a calling. I actually agree with them now, although I haven't always felt that way. My past inner battles with this mindset resulted in some self-inflicted hardships that, quite honestly, were unnecessary.

Their generation makes a strong case for seeing their career as medicine, but their job is merely a tool to be used to meet their holistic personal and professional goals and needs. Thus, well-being and self-care supersede their loyalty to employers and patients alike.

PATIENTS ARE THE MAIN THING

All generations of doctors know that the most important component of your job that will fuel your satisfying sense of purpose and meaning is derived outside of yourself and is connected to taking care of patients. They provide you with a daily surge of cerebral dopamine associated with the internal satisfaction you experience from helping them. Many of you chose this career to help those in need. Each patient's story and life are diverse, and your ability to enter their world and do good for them is what makes medicine so unique and special. Your patients are what will enrich your medical work as the years go by. This doesn't mean you have to live by the age-old mantra of "patients come first." In fact, you must love yourself first.[18] The continuous self-denial of your well-being can be disastrous, especially if you have no boundaries with patients and their access to you.

How doctors interact with their patients has changed drastically in the last few decades. In the years past, patients were aligned with doctors in a free market process that was driven by relationships, reputation, experiences, and economics. In today's marketplace, patients are commoditized, and corporations control patients' interaction with their system assets, in particular, their employed physicians.

In this paradigm, patient loyalty is aligned with a corporate brand and not with you. Thus, you become a generic service line doctor that takes care of your employer's other purchased asset, patients. This mechanical and machine-like environment tends to erode the heart and soul out of medicine over time and can wear down your sense of purpose and meaning in providing medical care.

This is just one of the many reasons that burnout has become an increasingly common problem for physicians of all generations. It's also a reason that one of the coping skills that many doctors have chosen for combating burnout is to depersonalize their work and frame it as just a job.

According to a 2020 report by Medscape, Millennials are much more adept at embracing this mindset and, thus, suffer only a

---

18 "A Guide to Practicing Self-Care with Mindfulness," Mindful, accessed November 27, 2022, *https://www.mindful.org/a-guide-to-practicing-self-care-with-mindfulness/*.

38 percent burnout rate, while their Generation X counterparts come in at a 48 percent burnout rate.[19] As I said, my Generation X cohort has much that we can learn from the younger generation of doctors.

In the end, the corporate ownership of medicine creates separation between doctors and patients that today is signaled by the computer in the exam room. This glorified corporate cash register is just another business tool that is interjected between you and the patients. In the long run, I want to remind you that anything you can do to touch patients, remove distractions in the clinical space, and maximize your face-to-face time with patients will ultimately make you more satisfied as a doctor. Patients—not operating your employer's business equipment—are why most of you spent the first thirty years of your life preparing to become a doctor.

The truth is that the healthcare playing field is now controlled by large corporations. It's a landscape that is heavily defined and regulated by the government and increasingly requires the deep pockets of large companies to operate within. The ownership of this space is dominated by big businesses that create attractive environments to lure in doctors and patients alike.

Healthcare corporations have kindly created environments for doctors to work within that they call safe harbors (Figure 2.2). I have been employed within one of these harbors virtually my entire medical career. This is now the most typical job structure for you to practice medicine and is overwhelmingly chosen by new graduates.

---

19   Leslie Kane, "Medscape National Physician Burnout and Suicide Report 2020: The Generational Divide," Medscape, January 15, 2020, https://www.medscape.com/slideshow/2020-lifestyle-burnout-6012460?faf=1#3.

EMPLOYMENT IS BEST

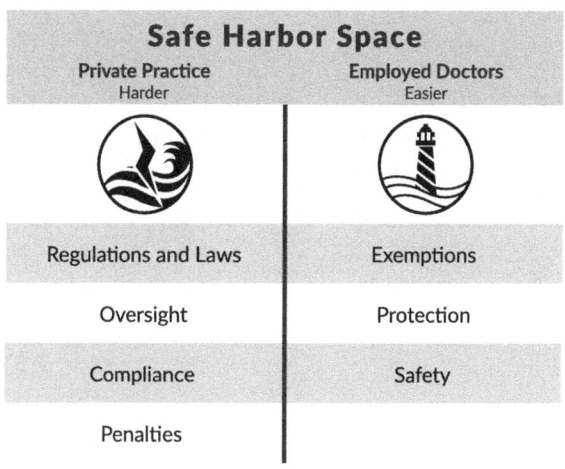

Figure 2.2

The term "safe harbor" is a legal term referring to the provision to reduce or eliminate legal or regulatory liability in certain situations as long as specific conditions are met. For you, it means you are Stark Law and Anti-Kickback regulations compliant, and your economic liabilities within the matrix of healthcare are limited.[20] In essence, it's a safe place for your professional services while your employer accepts the financial risks and compliance requirements necessary to navigate the uncertain landscape of healthcare.

Each harbor is a revenue-generating engine for corporations to vie for the growing healthcare GDP in the US. Basically, they are

---

20 Matthew Kreiser, "'Safe Harbor' Exceptions, Common Infractions, and Legislative Updates to the Anti-Kickback Statute and Stark Law," *Healthcare Blog Series*, JD Supra, November 12, 2020, https://www.jdsupra.com/legalnews/healthcare-blog-series-safe-harbor-49073/.

trying to tap into the $4.1 trillion pie, which is represented by the average of $12,530 that each person spends every year on medical services.[21]

The economic opportunity is so high that non-healthcare entities—like private equity firms—are now jumping into the mix to buy up small medical businesses as well. Now both of these powerful stakeholders are eliminating their small business competitors through a series of takeovers and buyouts. This is one of the reasons that you are seeing private practices vanish from the landscape.

These forces all add up to a pretty simple directive for doctors. It is safest and easiest to enter the workplace as an employee of a current healthcare entity that manages all of the ever-changing regulatory compliance for you.

PROBLEMS WILL COME

Although employment does provide you with a safe harbor, it does not insulate you from professional challenges. Problems will arise, and you would be wise to anticipate them and proactively try to avoid them.

Unfortunately, after the honeymoon phase of employment wraps up in the first few years, your job will likely cause some problems for you, especially if you are passive about managing things. For example, the growth and maturation of your medical

---

[21] "National Health Expenditure Data: Historical," Centers for Medicare and Medicaid Services, last modified December 15, 2021, https://www.cms.gov/Research-Statistics-Data-and-Systems/Statistics-Trends-and-Reports/NationalHealthExpendData/NationalHealthAccountsHistorical.

practice will almost always result in more encroachment on your time and force you to skip lunch, come in early, stay late, or bring home work.

On top of this, there are also unique pressures that employed doctors will experience the longer they are with an organization. You will begin to feel pressure from your employer to contribute your time with non-clinical corporate citizenship roles (governance, community education, medical education, e-learning, etc.). Most importantly, you will likely begin to feel your professional autonomy eroded as your decisions and medical care become more micro-managed by all the third parties in your world, including your employer.

Learning to adapt to the host of personal and professional challenges that come during the time you spend practicing medicine is critical to resiliently overcoming them. I see Millennials adapting to these pressures by migrating to jobs that accommodate shift work (pre-defined work hours), which doesn't require call and continuity-of-care responsibilities.

In addition, many choose to work in locations with better quality-of-life indexes so that when they are off work, they can recover more rapidly. Also, the younger generation of doctors don't plan to work for forty-plus years like Generation Xers and Baby Boomers (born 1946–1964) did as a result of their inability to disconnect their personal and professional identities from work.

In contrast, Millennials and Gen Zers are much more adept at embracing and developing their non-medical identity and see the high income of medicine as a method for more rapidly reaching personal goals like financial independence.

This should not be construed as an abandonment of their altruistic desire to help people medically but should be understood as a more holistic arc that demonstrates relational values outside of medicine. Baby Boomers and Gen Xers can be particularly critical that Millennials and Gen Zers are less dedicated doctors, but I disagree and consider them wisely reactive to the shifting culture of medicine.

This shift to large corporations controlling the healthcare playing field is why it's essential for all doctors to proactively develop personal strategies that will allow them to thrive resiliently during the thirty years (give or take) of their professional careers. Unfortunately, Generation X physicians are much less adaptable to these changes and, thus, struggle more with burnout. Rather than criticize Millennials and Gen Zers, Gen X doctors should observe the younger generation's self-care and well-being strategies and learn from them. This is best seen from the 20,000-foot view of your professional life.

THE BIG PICTURES:
THREE STAGES, TWO PLATEAUS

Figure 2.3

To help organize your mindset, I believe it's helpful to envision your career within the big picture view (Figure 2.3).

Generally, your life as a doctor is divided into three stages, each roughly lasting about thirty years. Bracketing the middle stage are two plateaus in a doctor's life. One is your arrival as an attending physician, and the other is your arrival at financial independence (FI for short). To successfully arrive at either plateau requires extraordinary determination, focus, and sacrifice.

Stage 1: Training

The first thirty-year space is generally considered a time when your mindset is assembled. This path to becoming an attending physician is a long and challenging process and is filled with clearly defined mile markers. Here others control you and determine whether you are ready to move on to the next stage.

Stage 1 is the space where your time and resources that are associated with your professional training all add up to formulate an investment in yourself. It involves a laborious, relatively rigid, and expensive creation of personal and professional assets that you will use to fuel Stages 2 and 3. The mindsets that you create here will heavily influence your views of time, money, and life in each of these spaces. It will also affect how you view your earned assets that are used in all three stages.

ATTENDING PHYSICIAN PLATEAU

Arriving at the first plateau is an exciting moment in your career. You are now officially an independent physician! Entry into the attending physician world is coronated by multiple federal, state, and national entities, like your specialty board, which affirm your professional status, and also require ongoing monitoring as proof of your continued worthiness. Only physicians and their close relationships fully appreciate the sacrifice and hardship connected to arriving at and maintaining this coveted place.

Stage 2: Professional Life

The highly diverse space in between the two plateaus is called your professional life, and this space is the focus of this book.

My goal is not to tell you what to do to create the life you love as a doctor but to forecast what you are entering into and help you thrive there.

If you proactively assemble your tangible and intangible assets into a highly individualized structure, they will help propel you towards your self-defined best life. This structure will be unique to your skills, needs, and life. No two systems will be identical, although the general architecture may look similar. This individuation process is another earned component associated with being a physician. You have earned the right to forge your unique identity within medicine, whether that be your choice of specialty or how you spend your time at work and play.

This stage is characterized by change and is highly dynamic as you independently live your life and encounter various life events that further define your identity. Beginning a family and figuring out how to parent and manage an increasingly complicated life is just one example of the complexity of this stage.

During these days, I lost my first wife to breast cancer in her early thirties, remarried, had five children, one of whom is autistic, changed jobs, moved four times, built a new home, and got nine businesses off the ground. Every one of these elements was filled with both hardships and triumphs. Life has a way of creating unique challenges and difficulties for each of us.

For doctors, the middle thirty years comprise a host of decision trees that are all pretty common to our tribe. All are "first-world problems," and all have financial metrics that will serve as separators of the length of time you will spend here and how enjoyable it will be for you.

In contrast to the journey to your first plateau, the journey to financial independence is much more subjective. It includes multiple personal and professional variables, which you primarily get to decide for yourself. Even the definition of financial independence (FI) is determined mainly by your self-determined present and future lifestyle.

Financial independence is commonly defined as having enough income to pay one's living expenses for the rest of one's life without having to be employed or dependent on others.

As the accompanying chart on financial stages (2.4) demonstrates, most of you will prefer to reach the place called Financial Freedom rather than Financial Independence because it will allow you to live the revved-up lifestyle that you have become accustomed to as a doctor. So as I reference FI in this book, it represents the minimum stage you must reach in order to not have to be employed.

FINANCIAL INDEPENDENCE PLATEAU

Progressive Financial Stages

Financial Security
Living with your needs being met with a confidence that your work income will meet those needs. Precious things are protected.

Financial Flexibility
Affording extras in life that are not dependent on your work; these items are connected to your savings. Income exceeds expenses.

Financial Independence
You can now afford to live at your *current lifestyle* without working any longer. Debt is eliminated.

Financial Freedom
You have accumulated the net worth that will allow you to live at the *chosen lifestyle* that you prefer for the rest of your life without having to work again. Investments are diverse and growing and lead to your preferred way of life.

Financial Autonomy
You have enough resources to do anything you want, anytime you want. You are free to live life on your terms without having to work. You have trans-generational freedom.

Figure 2.4

Not being employed has become a significant talking point among doctors of all ages due to the burnout crisis that has been accelerated by physician employment within the American health system.[22]

Most Baby Boomers are already moving towards retirement from work as the natural progression of their long-term plan to retire around the traditional age of sixty-five. Thus, reacting to the pressures of medicine is easier because they can just stop working a few years early. The exception is those who have financial obligations that drive them or those who are driven by their altruistic love for helping people.

Millennials and Gen Zers, as I noted, have wisely adapted to the new landscape and their entry and exit from medicine are measured, paced, and more actively managed. As a result, thirty-year sustained careers will likely be less common for them, and part-time work or even periodic work (like locums work) will be more normative due to their desire for balance and personal well-being.

My dear Gen X peers (I am one of you), you are, unfortunately, in the ugly middle. Many of you feel trapped because of your inability to step away from medicine for financial reasons. At the same time, you feel maxed out in your ability to endure your employer's erosion of your professional autonomy.

You may have experienced the good old days of private practice, the pre-electronic health record era, or the times when patients and doctors made medical decisions rather than insurance

---

22 Lorna Collier, "7 Reasons Doctors Are Leaving Medicine," Healthgrades for Professionals, September 30, 2022, https://www.healthgrades.com/pro/7-reasons-doctors-are-leaving-medicine.

making those decisions for both parties. This makes the present pain of professional life all the more difficult because you have experienced a better version of a doctor's life. Unfortunately, you are stuck, or at least you feel you are. Many of you are looking for exit options that relieve medical employment difficulties.[23] Sadly for some, that even includes suicide, with an average of three hundred physicians completing suicide each year.[24]

Regardless of their current age or state, I applaud and affirm anyone who is willing to proactively organize a personal and professional plan that helps them reach their best life. The old expression that failing to plan is akin to planning to fail has a lot of truth in it when it comes to your professional life. As you'll see later, I am a Gen X doctor who was able to adapt mid-career, and I am now thriving, having arrived at the FI plateau. Regardless of your generation, you can arrive here faster if you follow my lead.

Stage 3: Freedom

In Stage 3, your independence is maximized as you achieve independence through your assets. Stage 3 is represented by a financial state in which you are emancipated from having to work. Here, you are able to enjoy your earned assets as you manage them to fuel the non-monetized use of your time that is typically filled with what means most to you.

---

23 Jennifer Abbasi, "Pushed to Their Limits, 1 in 5 Physicians Intends to Leave Practice," *JAMA* 327, no. 15 (2022): 1435–1437, https://doi.org/10.1001/jama.2022.5074.

24 American Foundation for Suicide Prevention, "10 Facts about Physician Suicide and Mental Health," ACGME.org, accessed November 27, 2022, https://www.acgme.org/globalassets/PDFs/ten-facts-about-physician-suicide.pdf.

The last zone will become a space where you can decide whether you want to retire from any kind of work. Stated more simply, it represents a time when you can separate from being required to have a job. When you are employed, in particular, you MUST go to work, and your employer pretty well controls you—your income, benefits, schedule, and vacation time. But if you reach FI and no longer have to have a job, you now have complete control to determine if you work, how you work, when you work, what work means to you, and even whether your work needs to be monetized. Retirement doesn't mean that you no longer work; rather, it means you get to self-determine what your work is each day.

Here you can contentedly live a life whereby your desired lifestyle is met through your own financial reserve. This is age independent, as long as the financial assets mirror your life expectancy.

LIVE THE LIFE YOU LOVE NOW

By going over this architecture of the doctor's life, I want to help you live your best life and love now, while also linking this up to the life you want to live when you have the choice to work or not. Your personal preferences during Stage 2 of your professional life will ultimately affect the length of time that you practice medicine.

As an example, if you are willing to live like a resident for ten years, squirreling away massive monetary savings, this austere life will allow you to reach FI by your early forties. For those in this camp, the forty-plus years of not having to work are worth the "opportunity costs" of frugal living for these ten years.

For others, living a more robust current lifestyle with fewer sacrifices coupled with a rigid high savings rate might lead to being able to step away from medicine at age fifty. This less austere but disciplined approach hits the mark.

Then there are the rest who just assume they will eventually get there while living a consumptive lifestyle, trusting their financial advisor to determine when enough has been saved to retire, typically somewhere around sixty to seventy years of age.

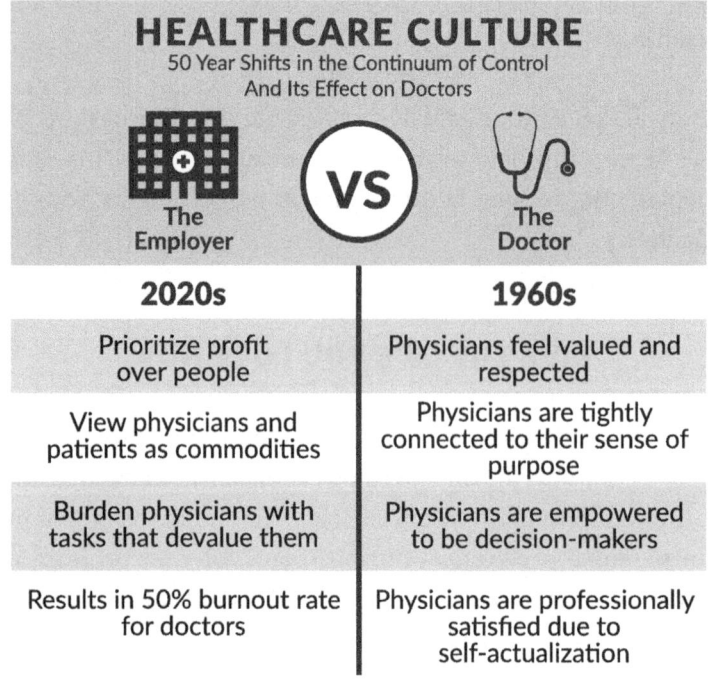

Figure 2.5

Which is right? The rightness is determined by your personal goals and preferences. But I contend that the unique pressures of modern physician employment, as depicted in Figure 2.5, reduce your professional lifespan, thus making you less likely to be able to withstand thirty to forty years of it. Past generations of doctors could manage Stage 2 for extended periods because medicine was more sustainable when they kept it under their control in private practice. Generation X and Millennial doctors must redefine the length and expectations of their career in Stage 2 as they adapt to corporate control of medicine.

It's vital to figure out how to live your best life as an attending physician now and not just fall into the trap of dreaming about the next plateau.

There is a risk of disappointment at each plateau due to what is called the "arrival fallacy."[25] Here, you falsely believe that once you attain your goal or reach your destination, you will get lasting happiness. You can avoid this empty definition of success if the plateau is not the goal, but it becomes the foundation for creating the life you love in that space.[26] Thus completing training simply serves as the foundation on which you assemble your assets in a way that shapes your best life.

Choosing to activate your power to start a PC is a crucial building block at the beginning of Stage 2 because you can connect your entire attending career to it.

START WITH THE END IN MIND

---

25 Tal Ben-Shahar, *Happier: Learn the Secrets to Daily Joy and Lasting Fulfillment* (New York: McGraw-Hill, 2007), 25.

26 Jimmy Turner, "TPP #5: The Arrival Fallacy," The Physician Philosopher, accessed November 27, 2022, https://thephysicianphilosopher.com/tpp/arrival-fallacy-podcast/.

Stephen Covey famously stated in his book *The 7 Habits of Highly Effective People* that one essential habit is "begin with the end in mind."[27] This particular habit is where I believe you have a clear advantage over the general population. After all, you have been conditioned to do this with a laser focus while arriving at the first plateau. For example, doctors are well known to be able to stoically deny and delay their social, physical, and psychological needs to maximize their focus on their professional work.

This conditioned behavior is elegantly demonstrated in the four burners theory credited to David Sedaris. In this theory, you must imagine that a stove represents your life with four burners. Each burner symbolizes one prominent quadrant of your life: family, friends, health, and work.

This theory conjectures that in order to be successful, you have to cut off one of the burners so that the energy can be funneled to the other burners.[28] And in order to be really successful, you have to cut off two.

You are familiar with this paradigm because you have learned to shut out virtually everything else in order to accomplish the hardwired process of becoming an attending doctor. During Stage 1, you only kept one burner on: *work*, in the form of education and training.

But as you start Stage 2 of your life, all four burners get turned on again. You now have time for the passionate pursuit of

---

27 Stephen R. Covey, *The 7 Habits of Highly Effective People* (New York: Free Press, 2004), 95.

28 James Clear, "The Downside of Work-Life Balance," JamesClear.com, accessed November 27, 2022, https://jamesclear.com/four-burners-theory.

the personal and professional life that your training has long delayed. Now you can open up all the burners to full bore, and your hefty paycheck efficiently covers the expenses as you start living the good life.

Unfortunately, this good life will often distract you from trying to self-define the next plateau of financial independence. That is because you may perceive it as too challenging, distant, vague, or restrictive to your preferred life. So you don't identify or track it, and thus, the plan to reach your FI plateau becomes poorly organized. In turn, the timetable to achieve it will likely get pushed further back by an unchecked consumptive lifestyle.

Basically, you know that you have a lifetime earning potential to pocket nearly $7–10 million.[29] Thus, you will eventually erase your debts, build positive net worth, and ultimately arrive at a point of FI. It's not a matter of if, but rather a matter of when. How you assemble and monetize your earned assets will ultimately determine the time frame of the when. The real question is how do you know when you have arrived here because the answer is different for every person. Therefore you have to determine this for yourself.

Honestly, it's not that difficult to come up with an individualized dollar amount that can serve as a proxy to help you know when you can stop working as a doctor. You can estimate this number based on your preferred lifestyle as an attending physician, and your annual living expenses represent that self-determined variable. Traditionally, based on the 1998 Trinity study, you can take your yearly living expenses and multiply them by twenty-five to arrive at how much you need for retirement. This

---

29 Todd Campbell, "Doctors Make This Much Money. How Do You Compare?," The Motley Fool, last modified October 3, 2018, https://www.fool.com/investing/general/2015/10/03/doctors-make-this-much-money-how-do-you-compare.aspx.

is predictive of how much money is required for a 4 percent annual withdrawal rate per year at your desired lifestyle.[30]

$130,000 Annual Expenses
x25

Your Retirement Target ➤ **$3,250,000**

Figure 2.6

The researchers chose 4 percent because you are unlikely to drain your retirement nest egg at this rate. Without getting bogged down in too much personal finance information, I can cut to the chase and simply tell you that most doctors will want to have between $3–5 million dollars in net worth to reach Financial Freedom at a doctor's lifestyle.[31] Figure 2.6 provides an example of this calculation based on annual living expenses that include not having to save for retirement, spending less on commuting expenses and other costs related to work, and having your mortgage paid off by the time you retire.

However, trying to imagine how your professional life wraps up when you have JUST STARTED TO WORK seems almost

---

30 Philip L. Cooley, Carl M. Hubbard, and Daniel T. Walz, "Retirement Savings: Choosing a Withdrawal Rate That Is Sustainable," *AAII Journal* (February 1998): 16–21, https://www.aaii.com/journal/199802/feature.pdf.

31 Ryan Inman, "How Doctors Can Find Out Their Magic Retirement Number," Financial Residency, accessed November 27, 2022, https://financialresidency.com/retirement-number/.

absurd. But I know if I can get you to pause and organize your mindset around this framework, it will allow you to enjoy the present and the future even more.

NET WORTH

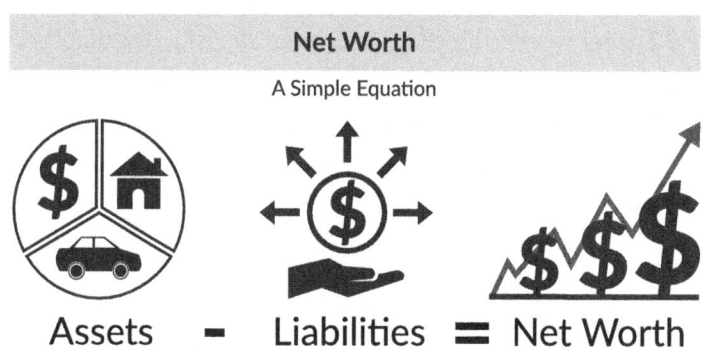

Figure 2.7

In order to track your progress toward reaching the FI Plateau, there is one critical variable that you have to understand, and this is net worth. This number will serve as the marker that tracks your progress toward reaching your FI goal.

You can track this personal number on your own, even though many choose to pay others to do it for them. Don't get me wrong, financial advisors and planners have their roles, but this critical number is one you can understand and monitor yourself. It is calculated by subtracting liabilities from assets (see Figure 2.7). The easiest and most accessible way to keep a running tabulation of this number is on Personal Capital's website or app.

The reason that this number is so significant is that virtually every personal or professional decision that you will make in Stages 1 and 2 of your life will impact this number, for better or worse. Knowing and understanding this will provide you with a SWOT type of decision matrix that many businesses use for strategic planning purposes.[32] As you go through Stage 2 of your career, you should always ask yourself, *How will this decision affect my net worth?* This includes your decision on whether to start your PC. As I will discuss in greater detail in Chapters 8 and 9, starting your PC at the beginning of your career is one of the most valuable decisions you can make to accelerate the growth of your net worth.

For several reasons, in the first half of my life, I never considered what I would want my FI plateau to look like. First, it seemed so strange to think about wealth accumulation. Additionally, deep down inside, I feared thinking about money too much would make me greedy. My Christian faith informed me that the love of money was the root of all evil.

Social psychologist Erich Fromm once described this risk: "Greed is the bottomless pit which exhausts the person in an endless effort to satisfy the need without ever reaching satisfaction." Fromm was always at the back of my mind, and I wanted to avoid becoming consumed by greed. Not thinking about wealth accumulation was the easy way for me to avoid this temptation.

In addition to that, I loved working and could not even imagine myself not working because my core identity was being a

---

32 Jeff White and Cassie Bottorff, "What Is a SWOT Analysis?," *Forbes*, last modified March 25, 2022, https://www.forbes.com/advisor/business/what-is-swot-analysis/.

doctor.[33] Working as a doctor reflected my unhealthy obsession with work as a way of finding meaning in life. So it was even more foreign to me to track my net worth, especially since it seemed so selfish. Frankly, I still believe it is critical for each of us to guard ourselves against the endless pursuit of more on the net worth dashboard. As many studies have documented, more wealth does not necessarily correlate to more happiness.[34]

Another mental barrier that I had with tracking my money was that I couldn't reconcile it with my belief that a doctor's work was an altruistic calling rather than a wealth-building job. In other words, motive mattered to me when it came to why I worked as a doctor. Ultimately, I feared distilling my work down to a financial equation that would remove the purpose and meaning behind it.

Due to all of this, I never did figure out my net worth til much later in my career, which turned out to be a big mistake. So one of my messages in this book is to make you aware of the FI plateau and why it is important to envision and track your progress towards it from the beginning of your career. Knowing your net worth is fundamental to this process.

However, once you hit your net worth goal, you have arrived at the plateau for Stage 3. You now have the freedom to use your time and resources for anything you can afford. Your earned autonomy now facilitates the complete self-determination of your time and finances.

---

33   James F. Sweeney, "Physician Retirement," *Medical Economics Journal* 96, no. 4 (February 25, 2019): 12–17, https://www.medicaleconomics.com/view/physician-retirement-why-its-hard-doctors-retire.

34   Amy Patterson Neubert, "Money Only Buys Happiness for a Certain Amount," news release, Purdue University, February 13, 2018, https://www.purdue.edu/newsroom/releases/2018/Q1/money-only-buys-happiness-for-a-certain-amount.html.

I have a dear friend who worked in medicine and whose spouse is a primary care doctor with the VA. Once he reached his financial freedom mark, he retired before age 50 from his corporate job and pursued his lifelong dream of serving as a representative in our state legislature. For Jack, his autonomy was translated into a different kind of work with significant purpose and meaning.

Having the unabated freedom to control your commitments that are not colored by pursuing more income and material goods is a rich blessing. Control over your time, unrestricted relationships, and enriching experiences now become the fiber of your life rather than work, money, and things. This version of retirement is not based on arbitrary age, rather it is based on the accumulation of assets that allow you to live your preferred lifestyle while not depending on a job.

ADAPTIVE CHANGES DURING STAGE 2

No matter how much effort you make to choose the right employer and chart the course for what you think will be your desired professional state, it will change with time. Your life in year two or five of your attending journey will look so much different than when you started. It is simply the nature of this zone of your life as a doctor. The real question is how you will adapt to these changes and how supportive your employer is to those needed adaptations.

I can almost promise you that when you compare your first day of work to your workday in year three, you will feel like you are working harder to earn your compensation, your practice experience will be different than you expected, and you will be feeling the pressures of not having enough time for both home and work. You will be prone to blame your employer for the associated tension and will wonder if you need to change employers to fix this. In the end, employers are not the sole cause of this problem. Rather your lack of adaptive measures to more holistically connect your personal and professional needs is the problem. An employer can't do this for you.

When you started, you likely over-prioritized the importance of salary and job title and minimized the other elements that you later discovered to affect your personal and professional job satisfaction, including your autonomy and your business powers.

Deep down inside, you know the solution to your dissatisfaction is not asking your employer to pay you more money, even though this is the most common adaptive change pursued by most doctors.

Your first contract has already revealed that your salary can't buy happiness. Rather your long-term satisfaction with medicine involves using all of your tangible and intangible assets to meet your personal and professional holistic needs and goals. Navigating to this healthier view of professional success is the critical adaptive change you will need to make within the first decade of Stage 2 of your career.

Examples of Adaptive Change

In the first decade of my career as a traditionally employed doctor, I was soaring professionally with a growing group of doctors and an enlarging income associated with high productivity. I loved working with our group, which had grown to eight doctor-friends. We were highly successful and masterfully worked together as a team. Honestly, I couldn't believe I was getting "paid so much" to do what I loved to do every day. We were a great mix of older mature doctors and young, driven doctors with diverse personalities but were unified over high-quality patient-centered medical care. This career zone led to a host of learning experiences that are all part of the extraordinary life of being a young doctor. But underneath it all, I was slowly losing professional autonomy. I didn't even realize it due to my satisfaction with the ample compensation and my beloved peers I enjoyed working with.

But for a host of reasons, each of the doctors in our group came to the realization that personal and professional adaptations were needed. As a result, four members separated, with one choosing to retire and the other three choosing employment that better matched their career goals. This included one who went into academic primary care, one who moved into urgent care, and the other who went into industrial medicine. For each of these doctors, this adaption met their need for a better work-life balance.

This resulted in the remaining four doctors absorbing their workload and thus growing our productivity due to the sudden growth of the clinic patient panels. This made us outliers in the compensation spreadsheets among the other employed physician practices in our employer's network. Our employer feared this placed them at risk for a federal audit due to our sizable individual compensation. So to mitigate their risk, they unilaterally determined that they should set a cap on all physician productivity pay within our physician network.

In essence, our employer was saying to us, "Keep working hard on our behalf, but we are going to limit your compensation in the process." This did not sit well with us, as it seemed unfair and unnecessary. When we asked our employer about remedies to this injustice, they told us, "This is the new contract and compensation model, take it or leave it."

This forced the four remaining physicians to make very difficult decisions as individuals and as a collective group—we labeled ourselves the "core four." We could either accept the new contract, or transition as a group into private practice. Like most doctors, we believed that basically our only options for continuing to work in our community were: employment with our current employer, employment with a different employer, or private practice.

While we liked working together, staying together wasn't a hill to die on. We all enjoyed the community we lived in, but it wasn't so unique that we couldn't move. We liked our employer, but we weren't content with their compensation plan. This brought us each to the realization that it was time to break up and support each other as we each went on an individualized employment journey. Jumping back into the waters of a new job was a little unnerving for each of us due to the potential disruption to our families.

One person quickly decided and took a spot with our former partner doing industrial medicine with no call, no weekends, nine-to-five medical care, and no third parties to mess with. He would not have to move from the house that he had just built and decided to commute an hour each way for his job. This allowed him to avoid uprooting his family, which was especially important due to his school-aged kids. It was a simple employed physician transition of ending one contract and starting another. He was my closest friend, and the loss was very hard for me.

Another doctor soon completed a sweet deal to transition his primary care practice to a different hospital system thirty minutes away. They set him up in solo practice, marketed to his current patients, and he took an excellent salaried position. He, too, was able to continue to live in our community, without having to uproot his family. It was a seamless employed physician transition moving from one employer to another.

This left just the two of us with a patient panel that was built around eight doctors, then four doctors, and now just the two of us left standing.

The other remaining doctor was an outdoorsman and contemplated moving from the Midwest to Montana, but due to his Midwest family ties, he chose to stay. He added in a new gig as director of our local independent wound center, restructured his employment agreement to reduce his clinic hours (so he would not hit the productivity cap and could then do wound care), and bumped up his compensation with medical directorships.

I was now forced to a decision point. I had to decide if I still wanted to wear my employer's team jersey. There were many aspects of the mission and purpose that resonated with me, but there were other employers in the region who showed strong interest in employing me so that they could tap into my large patient panel. I had choices, and this turned out to be a powerful negotiation tool.

I'll share in Chapter 6 the path that I chose and explain how you can leverage the same negotiation tools, so keep reading.

PRECEPTS TO LIVE BY

As I wrap up this big-picture chapter, I am near the end of Stage 2 in my career. My words of insight emanate from someone who has been there and done that. I currently practice medicine in the same trenches that you do as an employed doctor. I fully understand the constantly changing nuances of your professional world. My words should serve as signals pointing you towards your best doctor's life.

Beyond this 25,000-foot view of your medical career, I want to share with you some fundamental precepts that will help guide you into living a life you love as a doctor.

First, I want to affirm that you have entered into what I consider the most incredible profession that leads to an extraordinary life of meaning, purpose, and lifestyle.

Secondly, remember to keep the main thing, the main thing. You entered medicine to help patients. Even if being a doctor is just a job, don't lose sight of the good you're doing by helping others.

Stages 1 and 2 of your life will be filled with amassing assets that are used to fuel all phases of your career but are particularly important to Stage 3. The assets associated with Stage 1 are particularly unique because they are more intangible and are associated with the personal costs of earning them.

Stage 2 involves assessing and understanding your earned assets and then assembling them in a manner to help you reach your personal and professional goals that all lead to Stage 3.

In the next chapter, we'll focus on all of the Stage 1 assets that you have earned and discuss how to best use them during your attending physician stage that ultimately sets the table for Stage 3 of your life.

SUMMARY

- Your professional life is known as Stage 2 of your career and is framed by your attending physician and financial independence plateaus.

- You should start Stage 2 of your life with Stage 3 in mind.

- You should know and track your net worth as a marker for arriving at the financial independence plateau.

- You should use all your Stages 1 and 2 assets to live the life you love now.

CHAPTER 3

YOU HAVE EARNED ASSETS

AN ASSET IS COMMONLY DEFINED AS A RESOURCE THAT AN INDIvidual can control, which has economic value and the expectation that it will provide them a future benefit. Many of you will view this term solely through the lens of tangible assets such as financial resources or physical property that you own. Unfortunately, from this vantage point, coming out of training, most doctors don't have many assets and instead are liability rich.

However, assets can also be intangible or non-physical. They provide benefits to you personally or professionally even though you cannot physically touch them. This important class of assets includes things like intellectual property, contractual obligations, royalties, degrees, and goodwill. Brand loyalty and reputation are also non-physical or intangible assets that can be particularly valuable.

Young doctors tend to be tangible-asset poor and intangible-asset rich. This is a very important and hopefully incredibly empowering concept to get your mind wrapped around. Generally speaking, Stage 2 of your career will be spent managing the interplay of the combination of tangible and intangible assets as they are organized to help you successfully land at the financial independence plateau.

Unfortunately, when arriving at the attending physician plateau, many minimize the value and power of the intangible assets earned in training. Your journey has been a costly investment in yourself, and you have been driven by a vision of what you believe will be the incredible life of a doctor. In your eagerness to start practice, which most commonly today will be as an employed doctor, you may not take the time to pause and take inventory of how your assets can help you at this juncture. Let me give you an example of this.

Abbey is married to a pharmacist at her hospital and jumped into employment with the same corporation where she had completed her training. The ease of the transition, the location of the practice, and her excellence as a doctor made her career take off rapidly. She is involved in leadership and enjoys influencing the culture of her physician network. But as the time pressures of practice and governance mounted during her first five years as an attending, she began to do a mental inventory of why she was so stressed and unsatisfied. From all external views, she was thriving, but internally she was disturbed. That was because she expected the same satisfaction she had observed in her family growing up, a satisfaction fueled by running a successful small business. She realized that she craved personal and professional autonomy associated with running a business, yet her employed physician job did not provide this.

She had heard about my conversion to a PC-employment lite contract and was interested in doing something similar. For her, starting a PC would unlock a number of the benefits that she had ignored at the beginning of her career. Sadly when she approached her employer about transitioning to a PC-employment lite agreement, she was denied. Because she did not want to leave her current job, this placed her in the frustrating position of having to live with the consequences of not proactively incorporating all of her earned assets into the launch of her professional life. As a result, she was stuck in traditional employment, and her only recourse was to make a very disruptive job change.

Her most significant misstep was failing to start her PC as she completed her postgraduate training, which was then interconnected to her unawareness of the PC-employment lite option. Sadly, this is a prevalent story for many doctors who are unaware of both their power to start their PC and the opportunity to use it from the beginning of their employment.

I had made the same mistake as Abbey but was fortunate enough to recover from it mid-career.

I want you to avoid making this mistake too. But, to do this, you must understand exactly what you have in your possession as you triumphantly depart from Stage 1 of your career and step onto the first plateau of your attending life.

YOUR CAPITAL

After your post-graduate education, you have professional capital (defined as anything that confers value or benefit) in your possession, including the combination of your tangible and intangible assets. Each of these earned assets will influence your path in the next stage of your life.

Not surprisingly, your tangible assets are typically modest initially and often overshadowed by your negative net worth. This is because your accumulated debt is so high that your liabilities easily outweigh your financial assets. As I will explain later, corporate employers understand this about you and will use their deep pockets to provide an easy solution to your awareness of this financial burden.

For our consideration, I have organized your earned intangible resources into seven general categories. Their combination is unique to physicians but not exclusive to our profession. Each one is worthy of your reflection as you consider your mindset, time, well-being, and personal/professional goals at your career launch.

They have all been earned by you and are the result of your hard work and sacrifice. Each one is valuable and has its own power for you to dial it up or down based upon the complex tapestry of your preferences during the next sixty-year span that will include the latter two stages of your career. They are not listed in rank order as their order of importance may vary based upon where you are on the continuum of attending physician life.

Since I am writing this book as though I am speaking to the younger me, I will discuss these from the vantage point of the early career doctor. The value of each is dependent on the individual, and their interpersonal importance will lead you to leverage each in the context of your job. The seven intangible assets are:

1. Robust lifestyle/High quality of life
2. High income (lifetime earning potential)
3. Professional status
4. Altruistic purpose
5. Options and opportunities
6. Intellectual property (your medical brain)
7. Small business superpower

As we break down each of these physician assets, there is no doubt that many will identify with each of them, and some will be more important to you than others. The composite of these seven intangible elements separates you from the general public, other professionals, and the rich and famous. They are what set you apart as a physician.

But before we look closer into these, it is vital to observe how they are being transformed by the current mass migration of physicians to the system of traditional employment.

NEW ASSETS IN THE CURRENT ECONOMY

The shift in the healthcare marketplace has made employed doctors a very valuable commodity. There is tremendous competition for your services, so to attract you to work in their safe harbor, employers have had to sweeten the pot by adding a few intangible assets that you can now acquire from them in exchange for signing up to work for them. These primarily include:

1. Job security

2. Freedom to NOT operate a medical business

3. Financial incentives

Your future employer will offer you a deal that includes a trade of your tangible assets (debt) and intangible assets (options, intellectual property, small business power) for access to these new assets. This will then be repackaged as your new asset bundle. Before moving on, I want to pause for a moment and break down the components of this deal because this is the step that most commonly leads to the loss of your small business superpower. It is at this precise location that most of you will make the fateful decision that you don't need to start your PC because you perceive it will not help you in your employer's safe harbor.

THE DEAL

Whether you know your exact net worth or not, most young doctors at this stage do recognize their enormous debt burden and are searching for solutions to erase it. This includes considering how you can take your intangible capital and use it in a trade with an employer who will give you access to their offers that resolve your debt. As you review your assets, you will likely be open to trade in those that you feel will be the least important to you as an employee.

On top of trying to erase their debt burden, many are aware of their business and financial illiteracy and will eagerly look for ways to fill these voids as they start their life as an attending doctor. This all adds up to a combination of needs and assets that are brought to the negotiation table.

Employers are very aware of your needs and therefore craft their deal to effectively meet them by offering to off-load the business responsibilities, provide a predictable paycheck, and then add in financial incentives that make it hard to pass up.

As you assess your stable of tradable assets, you will likely determine the ones most treasured by large corporations, including options and opportunities, intellectual property (your medical brain), and your small business superpower. Thus, they will be on the trade block. In turn, employers will bring to the table the desirable assets of job security, freedom to NOT operate a medical business, and their deep pockets.

Your intangible assets of professional status and altruistic purpose are simply thrown into the deal and are expected to be supported and baked into the new job. On top of this, the employer will offer temporary—but significant—financial incentives like a guaranteed salary, a large signing bonus, and loan forgiveness structures. Visually the deal looks like this in Figure 3.1.

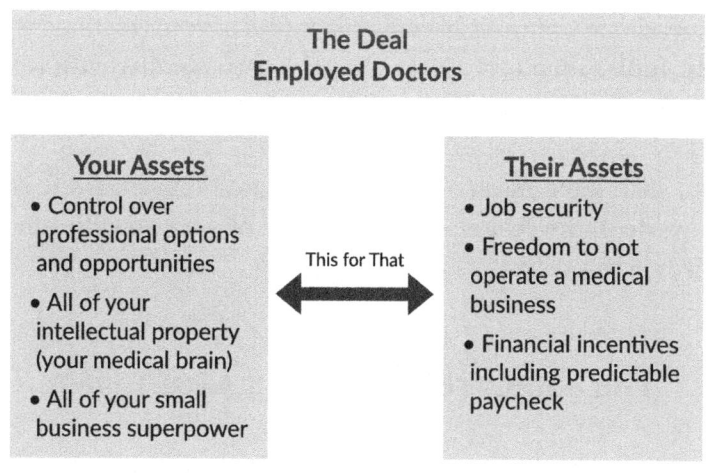

Figure 3.1

In sports terms, this draft-day offer will feel like a great deal for you. You only have to give up two future first-round picks and one second-round pick in exchange for three current first-round picks. In other words, you are willing to give up your control over your future assets to receive help now. All in all, the deal seems excellent to both parties because each side is benefiting from the transaction. On day one of the deal, you definitely feel like you have come out ahead with assets in your possession that help you flourish now by meeting your pressing needs. And, as I will explain later, your employer will feel like they came out ahead due to their ability to harness your business power.

The competitive terms for recruiting you are now framed by the caliber of your prospective employer's offers that speak to the intangible assets that you have held onto due to their value, such as high income (lifetime earning potential) and robust lifestyle (high quality of life). These now become the focal points communicated by recruiters in their headlines. Compensation, lifestyle options, quality of life, other financial incentives, and a host of professional promises become the topics of conversations with your future employer. Most of us are very familiar with these elements outlined in emails from recruiters.

Your distracted focus on these important areas makes it easy to overlook the relatively invisible loss of your small business power in this deal.

THE EMPLOYED DOCTOR'S ASSET LIST

Once you sign this deal with your employer, you will possess a new bundle of assets in connection with launching your career within your employer's safe harbor. This asset group tends to be smaller but is just as significant and includes:

- Robust lifestyle/High quality of life
- High income (lifetime earning potential)
- Professional status
- Altruistic purpose
- Job security
- Freedom to NOT operate a medical business
- Financial incentives

Ultimately, this modern grouping does provide a tremendous base for you to launch into a wonderful life in medicine, and mostly it's a fair deal. But it truly is a trade-off for you. However, once you look past the short-term gains of the deal, the long-term negative consequences might cause you to reconsider. It won't be until a little later in your career that you will fully understand the power you gave up to start your attending life quickly. Overall, I think physicians benefit from the early years of these deals, and employers cash in on the back end of the deals.

Frankly, most are so blinded by these irresistible offers from employers that the terms of this deal are easy to accept quickly. Many have no awareness that alternative exchanges can be made with employers, who certainly can't be expected to voluntarily offer a better deal. This entire step is relatively hidden to most employed doctors, especially younger ones who are no longer instructed in the business of medicine and are not exposed to many mentors who can help them understand it.

I am breaking it down for you now, so you can evaluate every component that is baked into your traditional employment agreement. At the same time, your awareness that alternative models exist, like PC-employment lite, will give you the power to intelligently negotiate a counteroffer that will better support your well-being and preserve your professional autonomy.

Before you blindly turn over your intangible assets in this deal, I invite you to rethink how each of them could be held onto by you while you remain employed. It is possible, and you have worked too hard to easily let go of their power to benefit you personally.

From my experience as a traditionally employed doctor who was nearly burned out, I know that restoring each of these assets back to my control was the secret sauce to my full recovery. In my healing path, I discovered an innovative employment space that allowed me to enjoy all my earned assets while remaining in my employer's safe harbor. This, in turn, reenergized me via the restoration of what I didn't even know I had lost.

As I will demonstrate to you later in the book, it is possible to incorporate these intangible assets into an employment model. I believe that your small business superpower is the most significant asset to negotiate, keeping it within your control.

TAKE INVENTORY

As you start to organize your life in preparation for Stage 2, it is very important to take inventory of each of the assets you have earned. This will allow you to effectively evaluate offers from prospective employers. But even more powerfully, it will help you determine exactly what type of deals you are willing to entertain. For example, suppose your priority is to use your PC for all employment job offers. In that case, you can signal to the recruiters that you will only consider PC-employment lite opportunities rather than traditional employment. In other words, you can define the categories of all job options you are willing to consider rather than having someone else define them for you.

So with this in mind, let's start by taking a deeper dive into each earned intangible asset that you control and discuss how you can maximize them as an employee of a large corporation.

1. Robust Lifestyle/Quality of Life

Your lifestyle reflects your preferences for a way of living that includes your place of living, your home(s), car(s), boat(s), vacations, and work schedule. The fact is that your high income will fuel and support a lifestyle that is only available to the upper 5 percent of Americans.

Your version of everyday living will likely be defined by the neighborhood or community you choose to live in, the friends you hang out with, and the media influences you expose yourself to. There is a broad and acceptable lifestyle range for doctors to comfortably live within, and it's up to you to determine exactly what that will be for you and your family.

As you dial this up or down, I suggest you maintain awareness that the higher you set your annual living expenses, the longer it will take you to arrive at the third stage of your journey, and the longer you will likely have to keep working. I would also warn you that it is much easier to periodically splurge to "live like the rich" than it is to keep your lifestyle thermostat dialed up all the time.

I like the way author Ron Lieber frames the lifestyle associated with high income in his book *The Opposite of Spoiled*. He says the very point of money is to be "grateful for what you have, share it generously with others, and spend it wisely on the things that make you happiest."[35] If you adopt this financial advice, you can modestly enjoy all the lifestyle components that make you love your life as a doctor. It will also help keep you from allowing a revved-up way of living to drive you towards feeling trapped by the need to do more work to keep up with it.

Quality of life involves both your free time and the geo-economic infrastructure that surrounds your life as a doctor. You get to define what elements are most important to you. Is it immersion within a preferred ethnocultural community that matters most to you? Is it the lack of snow? Do you prefer urban anonymity, or do you like being known by everyone like a rural doctor? How about what I call the "home triangle principle," which is represented by the drive time between your home, your work, and your children's school(s)? The smaller the triangle, the better it is for most doctors due to the time savings. Do you prefer the mountains or the beach? What about the distance from cultural centers that offer entertainment options?

The modern system of employed doctors causes physicians to organize their lives around "working time" and "time off." Your

---

35 Ron Lieber, *The Opposite of Spoiled: Raising Kids Who Are Grounded, Generous, and Smart about Money* (New York: Harper, 2015), 14.

time off allows you to anonymously assume a preferred lifestyle that can be detached from your physician identity, and many younger doctors like this. Your high income also fuels many options for pursuing interests that can be cost-prohibitive for the average person—like flying airplanes, for example. Many of you will choose your preferred employer based on the quality of life in your employer's community. I know this element significantly impacted how my son and his wife ranked his match list as he completed medical school. It similarly influenced my decisions about residency and my first job over thirty years ago.

2. High Income (Lifetime Earning Potential)

Most of you will earn $7–10 million at a minimum during a thirty-year professional career. This sizable annual income and lifetime earning potential is a powerful intangible asset that transforms into a tangible asset depending on how consumptively you choose to live. Fortunately, your high income will follow you wherever you go, and most employers are committed to providing a fair market wage. But some factors that will influence your income are specialty driven and geographically influenced, including the free market economy of supply and demand.

Geographic arbitrage is a financial strategy that involves taking advantage of the difference in compensation and the cost of living between two geographic locations.[36] For example, for many physician specialties, areas like the Great Plains will maximize the growth of your net worth because the earned income tends to be in the higher range, and the cost of living is lower.

---

36 "Geographic Arbitrage: How Geoarbitrage Makes the Great Plains Great!," Physician on FIRE, accessed November 27, 2022, https://www.physicianonfire.com/geographicarbitrage/.

Your job structure also affects your income, especially when taxes are considered (I'll discuss taxes in more detail in Chapter 9). For example, traditional employment typically leads to less household money than private practice or PC-employment lite models. That is because your business structure can lead to 10-15 percent more dollars in your household account after taxes are factored in.

Compensation packages from employers at particular locations can add significant financial incentives like signing bonuses and loan payback programs that can increase the total value of your compensation package. This may provide an enticement to land in a less-than-desirable quality-of-life location in exchange for more rapidly building your tangible assets and erasing your liabilities like debt (which results in growing your net worth).

Some doctors accept these arrangements whereby they/their family live at a preferred quality-of-life location, and the physician commutes or does block or shift work that meets the contractual terms of the financially advantaged job. Just a warning: these kinds of arrangements are rarely sustainable and can ultimately harm your well-being.

Income is such a critical issue to doctors that I will spend a great deal of time in the remainder of this book explaining how forming your PC and flowing your earned professional income through it can dramatically help grow your net worth. As I explain in Chapter 9, you will accomplish this growth via your PC because it will help you retain more income, enlarge your retirement fund, and diversify your other income channels through multiple medical and non-medical sources.

3. Professional Status

We are medical experts who still value professionalism and the special designation of being a healthcare professional. In your training, this is emphasized at the beginning of medical school via the "white coat ceremony" and consummated via a professional oath at your medical school graduation that commonly draws on elements of the Hippocratic Oath or the Declaration of Geneva.

Professionalism can further be described as a set of values, behaviors, and relationships that underpins the public's trust in doctors. Your code of professionalism typically includes:

- Integrity and altruism

- Pursuit of continuous improvement

- Commitment to professional competence and excellence in medical care

- Promise to treat the whole patient, not just their disease

- Commitment to honesty with patients

- Commitment to protect sensitive patient health information and confidentiality

- Commitment to maintaining appropriate relations with patients

- Dedication to improving the quality of care

- Commitment to social justice through improving access to care, equality of care, and joint distribution of finite resources

- Commitment to scientific knowledge

- Commitment to maintaining trust by avoiding conflicts of interest

- Obligation to first do no harm

- Commitment to prioritize the patient's needs over your own

- Commitment to caring for all people regardless of their ability to pay for services

- Commitment to make clinical decisions regarding the treatment and care of a patient without regard to financial or corporate influences

These professional characteristics are built into the arduous training process that each doctor endures. In a crucible mirroring induction into the military, you earn recognition as a medical professional as you graduate.

This was the goal of Sir William Osler, who standardized the training process for doctors at the turn of the twentieth century and elevated our professional status. Nearly a decade later, in 1910, Abraham Flexner's Report took things a step further to ensure doctors were adequately trained and equipped to care for the vulnerable through a standardized bio-medical model.

Of course, life in the twenty-first century is much different than it was during Dr. Osler's days, but becoming a medical professional still follows a similar pattern. It remains a standardized training system that uniformly demands a high level of commitment, humility, trust, and resourcefulness to complete.

The current traditional employment system downplays your professional status in many ways, not the least of which is by relabeling you as a "provider" rather than recognizing your position as a professional. Over time, this erosion of your professional standing within a large corporation will psychologically affect your well-being. The loss of your professional status is a pivotal ingredient in the slippery slope that leads to burnout.

4. Altruistic Purposes

This unseen asset sets you apart from others because of its association with your duty to always do good to your fellow man and your community. As mentioned previously, it fits in the Hippocratic ethical call for you to medically serve all the public equally, regardless of their ability to pay. You are an individual healer who experiences the satisfying joy connected with helping the hurting and broken through the art of medicine. This gives you a deeper purpose and meaning linked to your everyday work. It is truly special. Never lose sight of this guiding light in your life. It is one of the distinguishing features that separate you from other professionals.

Although the system might seek to break the bond between you and your patients, the simplicity of taking what you do know about the human body and skillfully using it to help others is incredibly powerful and filled with good vibes.

Regardless of the patient's social profile, you ethically provide care to all for the good of humanity. Whether employed or not, I encourage you to follow your moral compass and not grow weary in doing good for your patients and your community. Within large corporations, these altruistic actions are typically framed as part of your corporate citizenship since they usually fulfill your employer's mission. As a result, they are often expected and sometimes demanded, undermining your zeal for doing them.

5. Options and Opportunities

You have earned the power and autonomy to make the choices that best support your professional and personal goals. This is because of the investment you have made in yourself as a medical doctor. Of course, not everyone is so fortunate. This invisible asset comprises numerous clinical and non-clinical opportunities that will arise simply because you are a doctor.

What was unknown to me, since I was the first to attend college in my family, was that education and degrees are a gateway to life options and opportunities. Typically, the more educated you are, the greater the economic and professional opportunities you earn.[37] A doctorate of any type, including an MD/DO, is associated with greater exposure to all opportunities. Your high income and professional status are fundamental ingredients to arriving at this space of increased opportunity.

---

37 Isabel V. Sawhill, "Higher Education and the Opportunity Gap," Brookings, October 8, 2013, https://www.brookings.edu/research/higher-education-and-the-opportunity-gap/.

Your minimum of eleven-plus years of post-high school education provides you with a myriad of professional and personal options in life. This is not an inherited social caste system that you are generationally given. Rather it is an earned space available to any driven to pursue becoming a doctor. Physicians are not unique to this space, as many other professions share this unusual access to opportunities, including law, architecture, and dentistry.

Employers will recognize that options and opportunities are expected for you as a professional and, therefore, will wisely offer you an array of opportunities that keep you aligned and working on behalf of their system. They would much prefer that your marginal time be used for their benefit. Thus, they will place non-compete restrictions in your contract that will limit the extent to which you can use your professional services.

The power of having your PC is that you can much more easily use it to diversify your active and passive income channels inside and outside your employer's harbor. This places the control of these opportunities in your hands and outside your primary employer's reach.

6. Intellectual Property

Your medical knowledge is a powerful virtual asset that can be monetized in multiple ways. This represents your tremendous investment in training your brain and nervous system in the field of medicine. It makes you more valuable than the best that artificial intelligence (AI) can offer. You can powerfully display your intelligence through diverse dimensions and media formats, distinguishing you from AI.

For those doctors who work on research for pharmaceutical or bio-health companies, you fully appreciate the innate value of your intellectual property. But now, this virtual power has become the domain of the average doctor whose medical skills and intelligence have a value that extends beyond the traditional professional services that synchronously occur one patient at a time in a clinic.

If you are unsure of this asset, just look at the proliferation of doctors on social media who use their medical influence on websites, YouTube channels, podcasts, Facebook, and other digital spaces. This is indicative of doctors' earned trust with the public but also represents an awareness by doctors that they have assets that extend beyond a singular employer.

Depending on your clinical work environment, contractual restrictions on intellectual property may be legitimate. Still, there are times when employers may unfairly attempt to restrain your constitutional right to free speech and business enterprise. I encourage you to look closely at the fine print of your contract, read through your employee handbook, and then mitigate any overreaches from your employer regarding this.

7. Small Business Superpower

You are among a select group of professionals, such as lawyers, accountants, consultants, and architects, who can organize themselves as a small business called a Professional Corporation (PC). I will cover the details of PCs in Chapter 6. For now, it is enough to know that a professional corporation is a unique business structure available to individual doctors. It mainly allows the autonomous provision of your professional services within the free market and, as covered in Chapter 1, has a historical business basis. For generations in America, most doctors formed a PC when they began to practice as attending physicians. Starting practice as a doctor was akin to starting a small business.

With the progressive elimination of private practices from the landscape by large corporations, traditional PCs are becoming less visible and valued. Unfortunately, this historical transliteration of PCs and private practice has led most to believe that PCs have no utility for an employed doctor. As a result, many consider them dinosaurs on their way to becoming extinct.

However, as I will unfold through the book, your small business superpower can now be contained in a new virtual version of a PC. This more contemporary version makes it a powerful asset with multiple applications to doctors, including those employed. In addition, this reformulated modern micro-PC can now serve as the individual envelope for all of your earned professional assets. It can do so in a highly tax-efficient manner that is not tied to a single location.

This small business power turns out to be the central feature that every employer is after when they negotiate an employment agreement with you. This hidden element in the traditional employment contract "deal" will be perpetuated as long as you blindly allow it to happen. Your false assumption is that you must give up this power to incorporate yourself as a small business PC when you choose employment over private practice, and this is a huge mistake.

8. Job Security

Your work as a doctor is the critical business engine that corporate employers need to meet their business margin and mission.

Due to your critical role in the business of medicine and due to the growing physician shortage gap, you have chosen a career path that guarantees you a job for the rest of your days.[38] However, job security does not insulate you from job competition, as some positions are more difficult than others to land and maintain. Additionally, job security does not mean the absence of performance pressures that are corporately connected to virtually every specialty. For example, getting "graded" via scorecards your employer subjectively tracks is part of employed medicine's playing field. While performance is a normative process in the corporate world, it can feel demeaning to a medical professional like yourself due to its subjective and interpretive nature.

Regardless of your grades, your innate job security as a professional makes being a medical doctor a tremendously valuable earned asset.

This is how physician recruiter Merritt Hawkins framed your job security in a 2021 resident survey: 30 percent of final-year medical residents said they received 100 or more job solicitations during their training while 62% reported that they received 26 or more job solicitations during their training.[39]

---

38 "AAMC Report Reinforces Mounting Physician Shortage," news release, AAMC, June 11, 2021, https://www.aamc.org/news-insights/press-releases/aamc-report-reinforces-mounting-physician-shortage.

39 Merritt Hawkins, 2021 Survey of Final-Year Medical Residents (Dallas: Merritt Hawkins, 2021), 4, https://www.merritthawkins.com/trends-and-insights/article/surveys/2021-survey-of-final-year-medical-residents/.

"Physicians coming out of training are being recruited like blue chip athletes," Travis Singleton, executive vice president of Merritt Hawkins, said in a media release. "There are simply not enough new doctors to go around."[40] The sheer demand for your services throughout the US will give you a deep sense of security about your job.

This demand not only provides you with job security, but it all adds to recruitment and retention battles for employers of physicians. With this in mind, you have the upper hand when it comes to shopping for employers who, to win the competition for your services, will allow you to contractually use your PC with them via an employment lite structure.

9. Freedom to Not Operate a Medical Business

Most of you recognize your business and financial illiteracy. Thus turning over the management of the business of medicine connected to your professional services in exchange for a predictable, fair market value paycheck is a sensible and intelligent move. Furthermore, it is the right move for many to give up their small business power asset in exchange for this asset.

The decision to off-load the management of your support staff, billing, collections, and your interface with insurance in exchange for being able to focus almost exclusively on your clinical services is wise. That is because operating a traditional medical business does take time and can be challenging when done on the margins of a busy clinical practice.

---

40 Chris Mazzolini and Logan Lutton, "What Young Physicians Want from a First Job," *Medical Economics*, March 11, 2020, https://www.medicaleconomics.com/view/what-young-physicians-want-first-job?page=2.

Ultimately, this may be one of the most significant psychological barriers you will have to overcome regarding starting your PC, which is your fear of the time commitment and responsibilities you associate with running your practice. However, having operated within a PC-employment lite structure for nearly a decade, I can assure you that running your micro-PC is much simpler than running a complete medical practice, especially when you wisely outsource the business infrastructure and operations.

CURRENT TRENDS

Your inventory of these earned assets and their importance to your individualized personal and professional goals should not be your only consideration for thriving during Stage 2 of your career. You must also account for the ongoing market trends impacting your profession which include:

1. Increasing debt burden

2. Increasing physician shortages

3. Increasing burnout

I know I don't have to exhaustively convince you of these forecasts, but let me expound on each briefly.

Debt Burden

Stage 1 of your life is becoming increasingly costly, with a 2020 Medscape Resident Salary and Debt report indicating nearly 25 percent of residents owe greater than $300,000 in educational debt.[41] Paying off your educational debt weighs heavily on most of your minds. Employers and the government tend to have the deepest pockets to release you from this enormous burden. In most instances, this is a much more efficient solution than paying for it yourself. Thus early in your career, in particular, employment of some type usually makes the most financial sense.

Physician Shortages

Physician shortages loom as many Baby Boomers retire after age fifty, and the population overall is living longer. The Association of American Medical Colleges projects a deficit of nearly 124,000 doctors by 2034, including up to 48,000 primary care physicians and about 77,100 too few specialists.[42]

This shortage will influence Stage 2 of your career and give you greater negotiation powers with your employer. While there is a growing list of providers with physician-like capabilities (NPs, PAs, etc.) who will ultimately backfill these shortages, you will always have job security and a systemic need for your professional skills at the top of the heap. For example, you have trained nearly twenty times more hours than a nurse practitioner. That professional experience gap alone makes you a more valuable asset.

On the flip side, you are the most expensive employee for your employer. Like any business model, they will regularly contrive

---

41 Keith L. Martin, "Medscape Residents Salary and Debt Report 2020," Medscape, August 7, 2020, https://www.medscape.com/slideshow/2020-residents-salary-debt-report-6013072?reg=1#13.

42 AAMC, "AAMC Report."

systems that reduce this expense by attempting to replace you with less expensive help—like NPs and PAs that cost them one-third as much money.

The laws of supply and demand will also come into play with both urban and rural job opportunities, and rural locations are likely to feel the effect the most. For example, in the 2021 Survey of Final Year Medical Residents from Merritt Hawkins, none of the residents were willing to go to a community of fewer than 10,000 people; only 3 percent preferred to live in a community of 25,000 or less.[43] This rural doctor deficit will ultimately allow for geographic arbitrage opportunities for business-minded physicians.

Growing Burnout

Burnout is the most significant and threatening trend in Stage 2 of your career. For many physicians, burnout will force them to step away from medicine, jeopardizing the power of the earned assets in their life. The economic hardship of paying off massive student loans without the aid of high income would be an incredible burden on top of the emotional toll of changing careers. With an astounding current burnout rate of 50 percent or more, this has the potential to decimate your great life as a doctor completely.[44] The harsh reality is that this will cloud the future of a majority of doctors. Ultimately, it will worsen the physician shortage gap due to the early matriculation of doctors from clinical service.

---

43   Merritt Hawkins, *2021 Survey of Final-Year Medical Residents* (Coppell, Texas: Merritt Hawkins, 2021), 4, https://www.merritthawkins.com/uploadedFiles/merritt-hawkins-2021-resident-survey.pdf.

44   Leslie Kane, "Physician Burnout and Depression Report 2022: Stress, Anxiety, and Anger," Medscape, January 21, 2022, https://www.medscape.com/slideshow/2022-lifestyle-burnout-6014664#2

PUTTING IT TOGETHER

Your best life will occur when you can proactively use as many of your earned assets as possible during Stages 2 and 3 of your life. Therefore, I urge you not to let employment force you to believe that you have to give up any of them, but rather I encourage you to re-think how each of them can fit into your life.

This appeal to rethink how you maximize your tangible and intangible assets is a needed shift that involves changing how you view and value yourself. Then you will be able to evaluate how you can use your professional powers within the system. In essence, you must adapt because the healthcare system where you work will not likely change without any clear impetus.

Your most significant shift involves rethinking how the modern micro-PC allows you to keep and envelope all your earned assets. Your professional services will be at its core, and this physician-centric business structure will allow you to retain control over the many small business opportunities associated with your professional position and intellectual powers.

All the components for this needed employment innovation already exist, but they simply need to be assembled in a physician-centered manner (as opposed to an employer-centric manner) to help you hold onto your professional vitality. This architecture would provide you with the space where you can use each of your earned assets in a way that helps you thrive as an employed physician.

Thriving doesn't mean conquering the big corporations. Instead, it involves managing the relationship in a manner that allows both parties to work together symbiotically in a win-win fashion. One does not have to control the other entirely. The truth is that healthcare companies will not easily let go of their control over you.

INNOVATION

In the past few years, we have seen innovative changes within other industries, like Airbnb in the hospitality industry. Basically, they provided a platform for small businesses to compete with large hotels. Once they created the right operating platform for the unhindered interaction with consumers, the innovation ushered in seismic changes that made everyone winners. This included the big hotel corporations who still lumbered along in parallel with the creation of this army of small businesses that met the consumer's needs. There was plenty of space for both traditional and non-traditional systems to operate together.

This principle should inform the needed innovation in employment models, allowing you to hold onto more of your earned assets. There is plenty of room for these non-traditional models like PC-employment lite to operate parallel to their traditional cohort.

There was a time many decades ago that most doctors lived autonomous lives that were marked by professional status and were publicly viewed through their small business entity, or PC. While I am not advocating for a return to the "good ole days," I am encouraging you to assertively understand the breadth and power of your earned assets within a modern employed framework.

There is a critical need to swing the employment pendulum back towards innovative models that support your well-being. A sustainable future for doctors in the healthcare system will need to support your autonomy and professional powers by including as many of your earned assets as possible.

OPTIONS THAT LEAD TO YOUR BEST LIFE

While systemic change is needed, you must take ownership of the parts you can control. This begins by exploring your professional and personal options when integrating your earned assets into employment so that you can arrive at your best life. Of course, you can avoid a lot of hardship if you do this at your career launch by proactively accounting for what lies ahead. But if you fail to do this, like in my case, you can still evaluate your adaptive needs at any point in your career and make course corrections.

Let me summarize a few steps that you should take to begin evaluating your personal and professional life, no matter where you are in your career. These steps should involve you and your significant other, along with your preferred professional support, like an agent or a coach.

1. Write down any life goals that are holistically important to you and your family.

2. Write down what you don't like about your current job.

3. Write down what your ideal job would look like.

4. Write down what your best life would look like holistically.

5. Write down your weak areas and blind spots that would benefit from asking for help from others.

Each of your answers to these questions will begin to build an individualized story that will require specific assets that will help you meet those goals.

Once you have done the necessary work to inventory your goals and assets internally, the next step involves digging deeper into understanding your value in the marketplace. But, first, you must know your worth and why big corporations even want you.

SUMMARY

- You should take inventory of the assets that you have earned at each stage of your career.

- You should rethink how you can use your earned assets to benefit your personal and professional goals and well-being.

- One of your most significant earned assets—one every physician should hold onto—is your small business power through your PC. Ideally, this should be activated early in your career.

- Innovative systemic changes are needed in the current physician employment system that leads to a 50 percent burnout rate. PC-employment lite is one such innovative solution that addresses the systemic problem of burnout.

CHAPTER 4

BIG CORPORATIONS WANT YOUR BUSINESS POWER, AND SO SHOULD YOU

LOOKING BACKWARD FROM THE PIVOT POINT WHEN MY PROFESsional crisis caused me to convert from traditional employment to employment lite, I now realize that several powerful bargaining chips were available to me that I had not recognized. First, I didn't know my actual value in the marketplace because I had completely allowed my employer to define my worth.

It wasn't until I hired outside consultants to help me assess my professional options that I began to understand my assets and value. Unfortunately, many doctors have similar blind spots in regard to their own marketplace value. Secondly, I had voluntarily hibernated my power to form my small business PC and, thus, could not even fathom that it could be thawed out and used in combination with my employment structure. Again, my consultants helped cast a new vision of this reimagined special power that I could use as an employee.

After converting to my PC-employment lite model, I began to understand the personal and financial benefits of small business operations. It became clear that my personal business unawareness had cost me a large amount of retained income over the years—$1 million, to be exact!

It's painful to acknowledge that my ignorance about my own professional assets throughout the early part of my career was no one's fault except my own. And it is difficult to accept because that money could have easily stayed within my household to build my net worth if they weren't unknowingly and slowly given away to a combination of my employer and the government.

Had I known then what I know now about my small business superpower, I would have used this asset at the start of my employed professional life. Retrospectively, it would have helped me avoid the pain of near burnout by preserving my autonomy. Additionally, it would have placed me in a position to retire much earlier than my current projected retirement age of sixty.

My message is that you can avoid burnout, keep more of your hard-earned money, and reach financial independence faster if you start your attending physician life knowing that you are a business.

Your small business superpower represents the most coveted asset that every employer wants from you. Your business power is the primary reason they are interested in you.

WHY BIG CORPORATIONS WANT YOU

Simply put, you make money for your employer, which is why they love you. It's not personal, it's just business. Never mistake the reasons they like you for having any relational importance or social capital. Although you might be friends with some of the administrators or genuinely connect with your clinic manager, this is not why the corporation values you. Those are simply relationships of convenience, and they carry little corporate value.

On average, you, as an individual doctor, will bring in $2.4 million annually in net revenue for your employer. Depending on your specialty, this could be less or more.

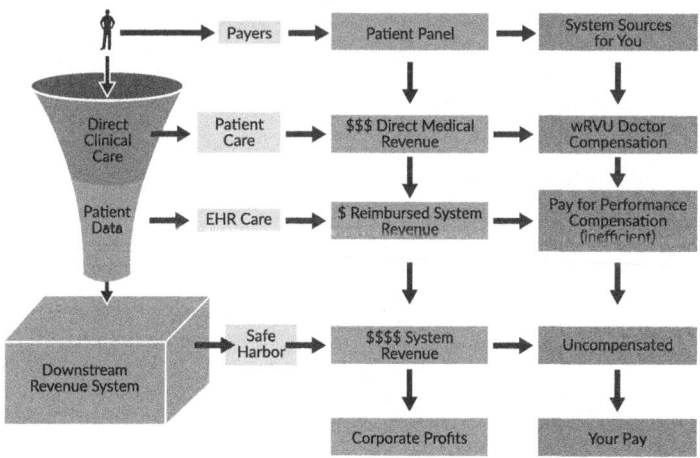

Figure 4.1

Figure 4.1 illustrates how money flows within the economic web of patients, employers, and providers—then how the health system makes money through your work within this matrix. The middle column adds up to create corporate profits, and the Dr

Income column adds up to become your compensation. Both the Corporate Revenue and Dr Income columns are powered by the flow of patients through them, as patients are now commoditized throughout the entire system.

The corporation is responsible for creating and sourcing the patient panels for you. Your employer will compensate you for your professional skills, the small business superpower that is connected to your individual work, and the associated downstream revenue generated by that work.

You will note, however, that your downstream revenue cannot be used to compensate you due to Stark and Anti-Kickback laws. By controlling your business power, your employer can harness your economic engine in three ways to create profit:

1. **Your direct patient care.** This represents the face-to-face work that you do with patients and generates reimbursable revenue through your professional services.

2. **Your EHR Data.** Your population health and quality metrics are **reimbursable patient data.** Converting this data to revenue requires you to make the information mineable within the EHR for a host of employer associates whose task is to convert it to money for your employer. This is the new oil for corporations seeking to squeeze every monetized drop out of their professional services.

3. **Your downstream revenue.** This represents the sum of money that your patients generate for your system as you direct and perform their care through the system. You are attributed ownership of your patient's movement, and your employer tracks that credit. Your

employer's goal for both patient and doctor is to avoid system leakage, which means that patients receive care outside of their system. The less leakage, the more money they make, and the more you are loved as a great corporate citizen.

The newest revenue lane is mineable data, which has been ushered in by the digital era of electronic records. It has proven to be a burden too heavy to bear for many individual doctors. It is almost suffocating to most. As you may know, it destroys your productivity and separates you further from patients via the computer screen. The result is a drag on a your day-to-day work efficiency, all while forcing you to work harder to maintain your expected work productivity income. Your electronic work is minimally compensated and is considered an expected investment of your time. Additively this becomes a force that drains your energy and professional vitality.

YOU WILL LOSE MONEY

In private practice, the business must make enough money to cover expenses, including the owner's salary. The hope and expectation is that it will have some profit left over to put back into the company or to provide the owner(s) with a distribution(s). If there are losses, those are usually covered by the owner, who reduces their pay proportionally to cover the expenses, or the corporation will have to acquire a loan to cover the gap.

Fundamentally you can't have a long-term successful small business without profits unless its owners can afford to sustain the ongoing losses or somehow recoup those losses elsewhere. In private practice, this is most commonly covered through a combination of medical office building or real estate and ancillary services, labs, X-rays, and the like. However, regulatory compliance and medical practice oversight laws have made these avenues more and more difficult to use, especially due to the concern for physician abuse of these self-referral systems.

This is where large corporations come in. They can strip out these income-producing elements and relocate them elsewhere in their corporate enterprise system. This "arm's length" separation is much more difficult for small businesses like private practices, but it is possible for large healthcare corporations because of their larger network of assets.

By doing this, they and their physician employees can no longer be accused of self-referrals due to the "arm's length" nature of the referrals. This, in turn, creates safe harbors for doctors whereby both parties remain compliant with federal laws. This all adds to downstream revenue, which is attributed to your individual work. As you might surmise, some specialties have more downstream potential than others and thus are more coveted by employers.

With this in mind, your employer knows that your direct patient care in a typical clinic will lose money due to many medical and economic forces that include the relocation of ancillaries outside the clinic, dwindling reimbursement rates, and skyrocketing overhead expenses.

They also know that this will all be covered by the revenue generated by your downstream contributions and EHR work. This data is available and visible to them but not typically to you. The information asymmetry is framed by a concern that transparently sharing it with you will risk placing them and you in non-compliance with federal self-referral and anti-kickback laws. Additionally, it is unlikely to show up on the practice-clinic "accountability report" that they will regularly provide you.

Employers recognize the business connection to you individually and their operation of your clinical site; thus, they will typically "share the numbers" with you regularly in a spreadsheet format. The purpose is to help make you accountable and aware of how your work and its associated resource consumption in your clinical space all contribute to the bottom line. In some regards, this invites your ownership over the process and reflects the reality that you are indeed the central player in operating the business. However, within employment, you are stripped of all authority, responsibility, and control over it. And most importantly, for this discussion, your employer is unlikely to fully disclose the true value of your downstream and EHR work. Thus, they will not give you a complete picture of your worth.

Thus these spreadsheets filled with dizzying numbers can often feel like "blah, blah, blah," and you ultimately just focus on your performance which most commonly is measured in wRVU. This is a reasonable mindset when you consider that one of the fundamental intangible assets you received when you made your deal to become an employee was to have the freedom to NOT operate a medical business. You chose employment so that you wouldn't have to think about the business operations. Thus, it's no surprise that you don't understand the complete cycle of your professional revenue for your employer.

It feels a bit wonky to have the accountability without any power to fix the continuous loss of money beyond doing the one primary thing you DO have control over, which is your workload and the associated revenue generated by it. Within a closed loop of your clinic, this is a conditioned and natural response for most doctors who are familiar with success that is derived through hard work. If we perceive we are underperforming—and the clinic is losing money—then our response is to double down and work more to make sure we succeed.

I am explaining this to you for two reasons. One is that it will empower you to resist the false guilt of needing to work harder for your employer so that your clinic practice doesn't lose money. Their system is rigged so your clinical space will likely be a loser financially, but that will be more than made up for elsewhere in the system as your professionally driven work churns through their machinery.

And number two is to help understand that you possess a business power that your employer will leverage both visibly and invisibly. Your actual value to them will rarely show up on the reports they provide to you about your direct patient care.

Employers want access to your small business superpower, and employment provides them the legal proxy to own and use it. I am not saying this is wrong; it is just a fact. Medicine is a big business, and you are a small business asset that is connected to their business operations. Helping to make you aware of this business arrangement is critical as to why and how you can view yourself as a business. Your big corporate employer views you as a business; so can you.

Ultimately, your corporate employer will not be interested in your well-being as much as they are in your economic benefit to them. Therefore, it is up to you to take steps to guard and protect both your well-being and your financial interests in the system of medicine. This is best done by starting your PC and using it within your employer's harbor.

THE NEW PC AND EMPLOYERS

As I covered in Chapter 1, reengineering your PC into a virtual envelope is a game changer for you as an employee because it provides the opportunity to reframe how your own corporation can allow you to continue to work for a large corporate employer.

The good news is that your employer can still essentially own and control your primary clinical services via an employment lite agreement through your PC, thus providing them all the business benefits they want in your relationship with you.

This PC-employment lite deal allows them to still benefit economically from their system control over your aligned professional services. Thus they capture the full revenue cycle of face-to-face care, downstream services, and EHR data. This is a critical talking point when alleviating your employer's anxiety or fears about allowing you to start a micro-PC within their safe harbor. You will neither compete with them nor siphon off any revenue you would have generated as a traditional employee.

As you begin this conversion, your goal is to gain access to their corporate bridge that extends to the market outside their harbor. As long as you fulfill your contractual terms with them, you will be free to use their bridge for your PC to formulate additional income in this free market space. In addition, this architecture will provide a place to preserve your professional autonomy that is often progressively hindered on the other side of the bridge, locked down within their harbor.

PC-employment lite ends up being a win-win deal made possible by a newly-formulated micro-PC and the repurposing of an old bridge that used to connect private practice doctors to employment through a professional services agreement otherwise known as employment lite.

Honestly, your employer doesn't need to control, nor do they want to control, your other professional interests. Their primary concern will be whether those interests compete with them in a market or if they distract you from being productive for them. They will be fine if they have contractual reassurance of these two elements in your PSA and see your consistent productivity for them.

For any of this to happen, you must understand the professional assets under your control and your value in the marketplace. Equipped with an awareness of this critical information, you can build the personal and professional architecture that supports your best life, including being employed.

That architecture will involve your professional corporation and your job. This structure will allow you to preserve your personal and professional autonomy in today's marketplace dominated by large corporate employers.

In addition, you will have greater control over all professional services and business interests you generate throughout your professional life. Traditional employment results in the complete alignment of your professional services to one entity. PC-employment lite allows a more diversified approach that includes a primary contract job but more easily allows for secondary work with no conflict of interest with your primary position.

START FROM THE BEGINNING

Starting a PC right away and slowly ramping it up will allow for a gradual and progressive understanding of how to operate your own small business and fully appreciate the power in your possession.

Before reading this book, you likely didn't even know you could form a micro-PC and still be employed by a large corporation. Thus, creating your own small business to support your professional life seemed unnecessary if you were not going into private practice. But now that this myth has been dispelled, I hope you better understand why employers want access to your business powers and why you should try to preserve your control over them.

The PC-employment lite option provides a better structure for you and your employer to share your business powers. However, this alternative to traditional employment still allows both parties to hold onto the core features of your business powers that are most valuable to each. For the employer, they gain your contracted alignment and the ability to harvest the revenue from the cycle of your professional services. On the other hand, you gain greater autonomy over your life and control over your household cash flow on top of the diversification of your household income channels.

USING YOUR PC IN YOUR MASTER PLAN

Organizing and activating this asset before you arrive at the attending physician plateau will empower you to use it throughout Stages 2 and 3 of your career. The beginning of your career is precisely the right time to integrate a PC into your personal and professional life because it is a natural stage of change for every doctor. The re-shuffling and re-organizing of your life at the moment of launching your attending life makes it much easier to integrate this new idea into your professional and household architecture now rather than later.

A few years ago, I built a new house. With five children, we designed our dream house to include bedrooms for each, along with some common living spaces. We intentionally included a partially completed full basement in the design, allowing for a flexible build-out later in our family's life. In essence, the new build was created with a master plan that allowed additional stages to be added later. In time we added a pool, basketball court, and tree house and finished the basement to support our family's growing interests. This was much easier to do because we started building our house, knowing that we would later ramp up certain elements that were built into its design.

The same is true for you as you launch your attending doctor career. There should be a master plan architecture that allows you to thoughtfully add in personal and professional stages as the need arrives. I suggest right from the beginning that you should create the fundamental components that will support your path to your best life. These should include forming a PC, creating a professional support team, maintaining your well-being, and reaching financial independence.

These cornerstones will help you reach the great life you deserve as a doctor. Much like my new house was designed to flexibly grow in connection with my family's development, you can build your PC to do the same. When you start with it in Stage 2 of your career, you will be able to slowly and deliberately ramp it up in connection with your professional development. Much like my basic house looked much different five to ten years later due to the additions, so will your basic PC look different five to ten years after you use it at your career launch.

In the end, all of this becomes important because behaviorally, we know that Sir Isaac Newton was right about his universal laws of physics. The First Law states that:

An object remains at rest or continues to move at a constant velocity unless acted upon by a force.

This general principle is a reminder that an individual will continue to behave in their current manner unless there is an impetus to change. Humans are creatures of habit. The design of our brains leads us to efficiently rely on autopilot responses and rapid assessments of situations. This automatic mode is much more energy efficient for our brains. This all creates inertia, or the power to keep doing the same patterns, because it requires too much energy to change our ways. This same concept applies to your decision to start a PC early in your career and to embrace employment lite as your preferred employment option. It even applies to your general decision to choose employment at all. Whatever you choose at your career launch is likely to create professional inertia that will become increasingly more difficult to change later. Including it in your beginning architecture, even if it's staged, is much easier and more efficient than taking the energy to try to add it in later.

As you consider your best architecture, I will spend the next chapter unpacking why I believe a framework of corporate employment is likely the best option.

SUMMARY

- You possess business powers that make you a desirable asset for large corporations to employ.

- The modern version of a micro-PC allows both you and your employer to benefit from your business power through a PC-employment lite agreement.

- You should start your PC early in your career as a foundational step for preserving your professional autonomy and supporting your personal and financial well-being.

CHAPTER 5

RETHINKING EMPLOYMENT

WHEN I BEGAN WORKING AS AN EMPLOYED DOCTOR, I VIEWED myself through the eyes of the team sports paradigm. I knew I didn't need to be the star of the team, but I also knew my performance would significantly impact my team's success.

They needed me, and I needed them. The mutually beneficial nature of this relationship with my organization was reassuring. I could visibly observe my personal and practice growth, which coincided nicely with the growth and development of my hospital employer. We were both thriving.

My entire identity, purpose, and meaning were all wrapped up in my life as a rural doctor who was loyally aligned with the community's largest employer and arguably its most important business. This bubble was comfortable until it popped, and I began to see the ugly underside of my corporate employer. It revealed that my unwavering trust in their management of my professional life was misguided and ultimately detrimental to my well-being.

This negative experience did not lead me to unilaterally walk away from them, or abandon physician employment in general. On the contrary, there was just too much that I liked about employment that made it worth fighting for. But it did cause me to pause and evaluate my assets and my marketplace value. After doing this, I could determine how to best use each of them to my advantage if I remained with my employer. In other words, I was now going to proactively define my professional life rather than passively let my employer do that for me.

Overall, I still believe employment is the best job model for most because of what can be gained in "the deal," as discussed in Chapter 3. It results in the coveted assets of job security, financial incentives, and the freedom from running a practice. The benefit of acquiring these at the onset of your attending career is just too powerful to pass up.

However, my experience reminds me that employment will require personal and professional adaption if you want to minimize its adverse effects on your life. Thus, I want to make you aware of the upfront structural-systemic adaptations you can make that will go a long way towards enhancing your well-being. Sadly, these adaption options are hidden from view for most doctors and not included in the standard structure of traditional employment, which is the de facto starting point for most of your job offers.

In essence, I don't necessarily see employment as a mistake; rather, I see the opportunity to revisit the components of the unspoken "deal" and discuss how that can be redesigned and rethought, allowing both parties to have long-term success. The current design is flawed and results in short-term benefits to doctors but a long-term burden that is too much for most to bear.

THE NEW MAJORITY

If you are an employed doctor, you are among a burgeoning majority. According to a 2021 press release from the American Medical Association, employed doctors have become the growing majority over independent doctors. And 2020 marked the first time the share of physicians in private practices has dropped below 50 percent since the AMA analysis began in 2012.[45] Although data collected by the AMA demonstrates the continuation of shifts toward larger medical practices and away from physician-owned practices in the past decade, the magnitude of change since 2018 suggests these trends have accelerated.

"There are several contributing factors to the ongoing shifts in practice size and ownership that include mergers and acquisitions, practice closures, physician job changes, and the different practice settings chosen by younger physicians compared to those of retiring physicians," said AMA President Susan R. Bailey.[46] She went on to say:

> Employed physicians were 50.2% of all patient care physicians in 2020, up from 47.4% in 2018 and 41.8% in 2012. In contrast, self-employed physicians were 44% of all patient

---

45 "AMA Analysis Shows Most Physicians Work outside of Private Practice," AMA, May 5, 2021, https://www.ama-assn.org/press-center/press-releases/ama-analysis-shows-most-physicians-work-outside-private-practice.

46 AMA, "AMA Analysis."

care physicians in 2020, down from 45.9% in 2018 and 53.2% in 2012. The percentage of physicians who were independent contractors has been steady, fluctuating in the narrow band between 5% (2012) and 6.7% (2018).[47]

This trend towards employment will only continue to rise because the massive numbers of young doctors who are now choosing the safe harbor of employment will only increase this majority.

Healthcare employers recognize these trends, especially with younger doctors, and like universities that pursue blue-chip athletes, the frenzy of recruiting is in full force. Soft recruitment within the training institution begins very early as early access to resident graduates is considered one of the most coveted aspects connected to corporately supported postgraduate education.

THE BEST LAUNCH AS A NEW ATTENDING

With the rising competition for services, it's no surprise that, according to Texas-based physician recruiters **Merritt Hawkins**, the employed-physician model is gaining ground.

As a young doctor, you are aware of this marketplace change and don't have to be convinced to join it wisely. This is why more than 90 percent of new physicians said they would prefer to be employed rather than own an independent practice. Of those seeking employment, 45 percent said they'd prefer to work with a hospital. Only 1 percent said they want to work as a solo practitioner.[48]

---

47 AMA, "AMA Analysis."

48 Merritt Hawkins, *2021 Survey of Final-Year Medical Residents* (Dallas: Merritt Hawkins, 2021), 9, https://www.merritthawkins.com/trends-and-insights/article/surveys/2021-survey-of-final-year-medical-residents/.

"The days of new doctors hanging out a shingle in an independent solo practice are over," according to Chris Singleton of Merritt Hawkins. "Most new doctors prefer to be employed rather than deal with the financial uncertainty and time demands of private practice."[49]

The majority of new physicians—62 percent—said they prefer to practice in cities with 250,000 or more people. However, international medical graduates appeared more amenable to practicing in rural areas than US medical school graduates.[50]

This profile for young doctors summarizes that they overwhelmingly prefer the ease of collecting a predictable paycheck while performing a job for an employer located within the urban area. This is likely due to the quality of life and lifestyle components that were previously mentioned, as they are becoming increasingly important to young doctors.

THE MUTUAL BENEFITS OF EMPLOYMENT

Professional employment is a give-and-take relationship. Ultimately, your employer will use your professional skills and small business superpower to maximally monetize you to their benefit in the healthcare economy. You are the engine that generates revenue throughout their system. You will be viewed impersonally by them as an assembly line machine, and they will try to maximize their profits through your workload.

---

49 Phillip Miller, "Survey: Newly Trained Physicians Swamped with Job Choices," news release Merritt Hawkins, May 14, 2019, https://www.merritthawkins.com/uploadedFiles/merritthawkins_2019_resident_survey_release.pdf.

50 Merritt Hawkins, *2021 Survey*, 9.

Better employers will recognize your humanity and seek to support your well-being while they simultaneously operate your money-making powers at peak capacity. There is growing recognition by corporate employers that healthier doctors are better producers for them. This is in comparison to impaired, injured, and broken-down doctors, who are highly inefficient business assets for them.

Thus employers are increasingly motivated to support your well-being, not because they are concerned for you personally but due to their need to maintain the productivity of their purchased business asset: you.

In return for your acceptance of this deal, your job will provide you with a consistent, fair market paycheck, benefits, and time off work that will allow you to live your preferred lifestyle. Your mutual commitment and loyalty to one another in this business contract are time limited. Once you reach the state of financial independence, employment becomes optional, and you are free to separate from your employer's obligations.

Employers provide a safe space for your preferred lifestyle and financial goals to play out over Stage 2 of your career and allow for an easy entry and exit from the healthcare playing field. This relationship provides a clean, guilt-free separation from your work as a doctor, which is quite different from trying to wind down a small business such as a brick-and-mortar practice site that you own individually.

ADVANTAGES OF EMPLOYMENT

Like the rest of your peers, you recognize many advantages to being employed, and I agree. So let's review a short list of those components that make it hard to pass up.

1. Sign and Drive

You can sign an agreement that immediately leads to high income, a robust benefits package, patient access, practice overhead, operations management, and the freedom to practice quality healthcare through your employer. In addition, you get to decide where you want to live at your career's launch point, and the rest is provided for you. Then, after you are licensed, board-certified, and credentialed, you simply show up to work, and the rest is covered. I love this simplicity.

2. Predictable Paycheck

Receiving a large and consistent paycheck every two to four weeks makes you feel valued by your employer and also makes your family happy with its associated lifestyle. It is a balm to the years of delayed gratification and the smaller paychecks of residency. Regardless of the economic forces outside of your clinical practice, you have the peace of mind that you will be paid well, whether your employer makes a profit or not. Assuming fair compensation, the simplicity of having a large regular direct deposit in your bank makes this an easy choice.

3. Built-in Benefits

Beyond a signing bonus, moving expenses, and loan payback programs, most employers offer a benefits package that generously covers items like health, disability, and life insurance, as well as large employer-supported retirement programs. Moreover, these turn-key programs are sourced for you without having to sort through charlatan insurance sales forces. This is another huge win for you due to its value and the time it saves you from sourcing it yourself.

4. Term Limits

Most initial contracts are for two to three years, although it can be longer if there is a significant loan payback. Regardless, you know that for better or worse, you are not "stuck" in this job forever. Given that only 50 percent stay with their first job for more than three years, this is an excellent benefit to being employed.[51] You can dip your foot in the water and explore your employer's workspace without a long-term commitment.

5. Time Off

Whether you choose shift work or another blended version, employment allows you to predetermine your workload. It is hardwired into your contract, providing time off at whatever

---

51 Edward Doyle, "It Might Be Your First Job, But Is It the Right Fit?," *Today's Physician*, August 2017, https://todaysphysician.com/first-job-right-fit/.

threshold you and your employer agree to. Unlike a small business owner who is always on, you get to disengage completely after you meet your contractual duties, and thus you and your loved ones can enjoy your life outside of medicine even more.

6. Self-Awareness of Your Business Illiteracy

Finding refuge in the safe harbor of an employer and letting them manage all stakeholders within the boiling waters of the healthcare economy is a wise move. This is a welcome option compared to private practice due to its complicated moving parts. You can focus exclusively on efficiently taking care of patients like you were trained to do, rather than inefficiently using your time to learn how to run a business without any training.

THE DISADVANTAGES OF EMPLOYMENT

The fact is that every coin has two sides. So assuming you have embraced the advantages of employment, you are well on your way to being a part of the legion of employed doctors around the country.

However, I believe it's important to make you aware of the harmful elements associated with employment that are harder to see, especially in the beginning. They are often so indolent that you are not likely to notice them. I liken it to a mother of a newborn with jaundice who is so enamored with her new baby but also so tired and consumed with her primary task of providing regular nutrition to her baby that she doesn't even see color changes in her neonate. However, when a friend or healthcare worker views the baby with fresh eyes, it's often clear that the baby is yellow. What is evident to some is often unseen by the one who is intensely in the middle of the experience. My goal in this section is to use my experience as an employed doctor to illuminate what lies ahead for you, even if you can't see it right now.

While at your job, you will be asked to deny yourself and conform to the collective good of your employer. This corporatization process will eventually erode your identity and your sense of personal and professional autonomy. The associated loss of autonomy as a professional turns out to be a foundational source of burnout, should you experience it.[52]

The last thirty years have witnessed significant erosion of physician autonomy from its peak in the preceding "golden age of doctoring" (the late twentieth century and early twenty-first century).[53] Now there are escalating constraints on autonomy that have been instituted in the successive waves of triple-aim health reform that were meant to improve healthcare, including systemic initiatives like managed care, evidence-based medicine, patient-centered care, and value-based care.[54] Each

---

[52] National Academy of Medicine, "Factors Contributing to Clinician Burnout and Professional Well-Being," in *Taking Action against Clinician Burnout: A Systems Approach to Professional Well-Being* (Washington, DC: The National Academies Press, 2019), 101, https://www.ncbi.nlm.nih.gov/books/NBK552615/.

[53] John B. McKinlay and Lisa D. Marceau, "The End of the Golden Age of Doctoring," *International Journal of Health Services* 32, no. 2 (2002): 379–416, https://doi.org/10.2190/JL1D-21BG-PK2N-J0KD.

[54] Donald M. Berwick, Thomas W. Nolan, and John Whittington, "The Triple Aim: Care, Health, and Cost," *Health Affairs* 27, no. 3 (May/June 2008): 759–769, https://doi.org/10.1377/hlthaff.27.3.759.

wave has diminished professional autonomy and challenged occupational well-being.[55]

Now you know that your autonomy and well-being will likely be under siege as a doctor in the current system, but this will be especially true as an employed doctor. So let's take it a step further and look at some of the other aspects of your professional life that will be affected by becoming an employee of a large corporation. As we emerge from the shadows of the COVID-19 pandemic, let's start with the biggest issue facing our tribe: the burgeoning physician burnout rate.

50 Percent

One out of two is the startling ratio that should be flashing in bright red in front of all doctors. According to the 2022 Medscape survey, nearly one out of two physicians are currently experiencing burnout, with the rate as high as 60 percent for emergency medicine physicians.[56]

These numbers are astonishing for one of the most important professions in our society. This trend is still growing among the brightest, most driven, and most educated doctors in America. The COVID-19 pandemic has made things worse, as noted in the findings from the 2021 Survey of America's Physicians, COVID-19 Impact Edition: A Year Later:

---

55 Anthony C. Waddimba et al., "Physicians' Perceptions of Autonomy Support during Transition to Value-Based Reimbursement: A Multi-Center Psychometric Evaluation of Six-Item and Three-Item Measures," PLoS One 15, no. 4 (2020): e0230907, https://doi.org/10.1371/journal.pone.0230907.

56 Leslie Kane, "Physician Burnout and Depression Report 2022: Stress, Anxiety, and Anger," Medscape, January 21, 2022, https://www.medscape.com/slideshow/2022-lifestyle-burnout-6014664#2.

- A significantly larger proportion of younger (64 percent) and female (69 percent) physicians reported frequently feeling burnout as compared to older (59 percent) and male (57 percent) physicians.

- Physicians who were employed by hospitals or health systems experienced more frequent feelings of burnout (64 percent) as compared to independent physicians (56 percent).

- Nearly eight out of ten physicians indicated they experienced changes to their practice or employment due to COVID-19.[57]

It's worth noting here that younger employed doctors have been impacted the most, which is worse if you are a female physician. This finding confounds the pre-pandemic data on the burnout risks for each demographic group. The exact reason for this is unclear, but it would appear that each doctor's resiliency measures were overwhelmed by the global life impact of the COVID-19 pandemic.

Unquestionably, it placed heavy psychological and physical strains on the healthcare workforce, whose ethical call to self-denial and public service was maxed out. For those who were employed, this only compounded the already growing sense of pain that their jobs were levying on them.

---

57 "New Survey Reveals 55% of Physicians Know a Physician Who Considered, Attempted or Died by Suicide," news release, The Physicians Foundation, August 5, 2021, https://physiciansfoundation.org/press-releases/new-survey-reveals-55-of-physicians-know-a-physician-who-considered-attempted-or-died-by-suicide/.

The pandemic was an intense reminder of your internal drive and motivation to ethically care for the sick. But this was also tempered by the harsh reality that your employers expected and even forced you to work longer, harder, and at personal risk of losing your life to the virus. The resulting physical and emotional exhaustion was minimized as your loyal service was expected and required.

Many even experienced their employer unilaterally changing the terms of their contract or even severing it without cause due to a legal loophole commonly buried in the contract called "Force Majeure." This clause frees both parties from liability or obligation when an extraordinary event or circumstance beyond the parties' control—such as war, strike, or epidemic—prevents one or both parties from fulfilling their obligations under the contract. Technically this is a bit different from the "Act of God" clause that is also found in your contract.

Now, as the pandemic transitions to its endemic phase, many employers are finding it necessary to slash costs in reaction to the mounting losses they experienced during the pandemic. Unfortunately, these post-pandemic changes that are being experienced by doctors and staff feel like an act of ingratitude after their all-consuming loyalty to their employer during the pandemic.

All of these dynamics of work fatigue and the loss of well-being are additive to the normal loss of vitality that is associated with being an employee.

The Loss of Vitality

When you become employed, an imperceptible process often unfolds as your autonomy, value, and confidence are slowly reduced into the melting pot of corporate citizenship. This will ultimately collide with your self-identity and home life. Of course, you will do your best to resiliently block out these forces and embrace the good life that you and your family expected would come with Stage 2, but it will be hard to do this.

For the reasons mentioned in Chapter 1, self-employed/small business doctors have built-in autonomy that allows them to more aptly and flexibly respond to personal and professional stresses within the very dynamic Stage 2 of your life. In contrast, traditional employees lack this flexibility due to the progressive professional constraints they experience and the associated intrusion of employment into their personal life.

You may end up feeling like you have no energy. The mental and physical toll associated with your job can drain your energy tank daily and make it difficult for you to mount the needed forces to drink up life with your loved ones. In this state, your ability to enjoy life outside of work will gradually diminish. Time off will become a recovery zone for returning to the grind. You might be home with your family, but you are not present with them—your professional state has hijacked your self-identity and has begun compromising your well-being.

The inflexibility of employment makes this more challenging than for those who run their own small medical business. Tension points exist for both camps, but the self-employed often do not feel as trapped as those who are employed.

The rat race of your professional life may also cause you to compromise your personal health and self-care. You will tend to eat poorly, consume more alcohol, and neglect your body due to the personal margins that have collapsed on you. The time and attention needed to holistically care for your biological, social, psychological, and spiritual needs are overcome by the tyranny of a medical career's urgent and all-consuming black hole.

Your habits and patterns become a virtuoso of momentary experiences that seek to hide what has been broken down by your loss of control and self-identity. In the end, your body will break down due to these habits created by the relentless pressures of your job.

As it rolls on, you may begin to feel resentment towards your job. If it gets bad enough, you will begin to resent your patients, whom you will see as a never-ending source of tasks to be completed. Your negativity will then steal your coveted work-life balance, which can easily get out of control in medicine. That loss of control will begin to suck you into the vortex of burnout and loss of well-being. Some label this a moral injury due to demands that employers, third parties, and patients place on you; those entities, led by your employer, force you to act against your self-actualization needs. Thus it is considered a moral transgression due to the psychological duress.

All of this makes some doctors feel so overwhelmed that their only conceivable solution to mitigate the shame of failing at their profession is to take their own life. This is why today, the suicide rate among doctors is the highest of any profession, as one doctor completes suicide in the United States nearly every day.[58]

It is clear that there are systemic forces at play in these trends, and corporate employment is at least part of the problem due to

---

58 Pauline Anderson, "Doctors' Suicide Rate Highest of Any Profession," WebMD, May 8, 2018, https://www.webmd.com/mental-health/news/20180508/doctors-suicide-rate-highest-of-any-profession%231.

the multiple ways that it will break you down through issues like too many bureaucratic tasks, lack of respect from employers, lack of control or autonomy over your life, and EHRs.

The awareness of this risk is why some surveys indicate that one in five newly trained physicians expressed "buyer's remorse" over their choice of career. This is in part a reflection on the current turbulent state of the medical profession and the unsettled state of the healthcare system as a whole. "With high levels of physician burnout and continued uncertainty about the direction of the healthcare system, many doctors are under duress today," according to Travis Singleton with Merritt Hawkins. "It is not surprising that some newly trained doctors regret their choice of a career."[59]

With this threat being so menacing and life-endangering as you launch into your long-anticipated career, you truly need a proactive plan at the beginning that will help you avoid this dreaded space of moral injury and burnout. Regrettably, I learned this the hard way, as I passively leaned into my employer's guidance and found that it led me to a broken state. The truth is that although I was highly successful in my career, the slow fade of losing my personal and professional autonomy finally reached its tipping point and nearly overtook me.

The trend lines of increasing physician employment and increasing physician burnout mean these two interlocked patterns of employment and burnout likely have a cause-and-effect relationship.[60] Everyone getting ready to sign an

---

59 Miller, "Survey: Newly Trained Physicians Swamped."

60 Rikinkumar S. Patel, et al., "Factors Related to Physician Burnout and Its Consequences: A Review," *Behav Sci* 8, no. 11 (2018): 98, doi:10.3390/bs8110098

employment contract should understand the treacherous waters they are wading into that will infringe on their autonomy and self-identity.

The Effect of Subjugation

Professional Autonomy can be defined as *the quality or state of being independent and self-directing, especially in making decisions, enabling professionals to exercise judgment as they see fit during the performance of their jobs.*[61] Once you sign that employment agreement, you are now subjugating your professional autonomy to others within your organization. Beyond the burnout discussion, this subjugation process will have effects on your professional life within a large corporation.

This means you will compete with others for finite resources within your organization. Your staffing, equipment, and clinical support will be strictly regulated and sequestered to the annual budget cycle undulations. The capital necessary for your needs will be limited and must be shared in a forced rank-order process with other physicians, providers, and departments.

One pro tip for you here: your best shot at getting resources is during your first-year honeymoon phase when your employer is trying to impress you. Because the truth is that the next fiscal year, you will be circumvented by the latest newly hired star physician, because your time in the sun is short-lived with most employers. It's just how the corporate cycle rolls.

---

61 National Library of Medicine, s.v. "Professional Autonomy," last modified July 25, 2001, https://meshb-prev.nlm.nih.gov/record/ui?ui=D017009.

Your voice and influence with your employer will rapidly decline after you start. This is because you are now one among a legion of corporate citizens, and your voice in the organization is relatively unheard by the C-suite. You are now a small cog in a big wheel.

Your employer will track corporate citizenship behavior, and you will have to prove your loyalty to the organization's mission through your voluntary and involuntary work for them outside of direct patient contact. In essence, they like to see that you use your personal time and energy to help fulfill the organizational mission.

You will be especially tempted to believe that your voice and influence will be greater if you volunteer within the corporate governance system. Unfortunately, you'll soon discover that those meetings are time holes that are filled with chatter about decisions that the administration has likely already made.

Your decision-making power will become diminished through a constant flow of prior approvals and managed care, whereby your clinical judgment will be questioned every day by everyone, from patients to third parties that control medicine. This constant barrage will tear away your professional autonomy and is made worse by the rigid quality of care guidelines and safety policies that are commonplace with employers.

So, as much as you expect to be empowered with autonomy upon your arrival at the attending physician plateau, you will discover that employment is filled with many forces that will systematically reduce it.

With all this in mind, let's revisit Dr. Tony from Chapter 1. He had embraced an employed position but is now four years into the job. Over these years, the professional pain of being controlled, devalued, and commoditized as a healthcare employee has caused him to experience various degrees of moral injury, frustrations, a feeling of being trapped, and enough professional dissatisfaction that he recognizes that something needs to change.

During this three- to five-year zone, Dr. Tony also becomes more tuned into his personal finances, the business of medicine, his professional development and identity, his lifestyle preferences, and both the advantages and disadvantages associated with employment in the healthcare system.

This all converges at his contractual renewal, and he begins questioning his personal and professional future with his employer. He is aware that the longer he stays in his current situation, the harder it becomes to move, change employers, maintain his family's lifestyle, make more money, or make changes that improve his diminishing professional satisfaction.

Dr. Tony and his loved ones become caught in a vicious cycle of believing some adjustments at work "will make things better soon," but "better" always seems elusive because new issues always replace the old ones. Finally, he and his family begin to accept that this is the expected life of a doctor and tolerate it due to the high income and the associated robust lifestyle. Ultimately, Dr. Tony looks for side jobs to make more money or be paid more by his employer to fuel his family's growing consumptive lifestyle. Due to the additional work, he loses even more of his most valuable asset, time outside of medicine—which, in turn, further erodes his well-being.

RESPONSIVE STRATEGIES FOR THE PRESENT SYSTEM

Your life does not have to look like Dr. Tony's. I don't want to end this chapter by giving you the impression that the risks of corporate employment outweigh the benefits. I don't think they do, but I know it's important to transparently communicate with you and forecast the potential hazards you will encounter as part of your decision. Understanding these elements will give you a better perspective on the proactive professional adaptations you will need to make to avoid these challenges and ultimately love your life as a doctor.

Your attention should be drawn to strategies that foster your well-being via enhanced support for professional autonomy. An excellent example of this is the Quadruple Aim initiative, which focuses attention on the care of you as a healthcare professional.[62]

As you likely know, Triple Aim has been widely adopted by healthcare employers and involves the threefold focus of enhancing patient experience, improving population health, and reducing cost.[63] These are broadly accepted as a blueprint to improve health system performance. Sadly, doctors and staff tend to be commoditized by employers in this model, and the result of that philosophy is the widespread burnout and dissatisfaction of the healthcare workforce.

---

62 Thomas Bodenheimer and Christine Sinsky, "From Triple to Quadruple Aim: Care of the Patient Requires Care of the Provider," *The Annals of Family Medicine* 12, no. 6 (November 2014): 573–576, https://doi.org/10.1370/afm.1713.

63 Berwick, Nolan, and Whittington, "The Triple Aim," 760.

The Quadruple Aim adds back a critical component that focuses on improving the work life of healthcare providers, including clinicians and staff. In this model, your well-being is elevated as a priority for the efficient operation of the healthcare system. While this often includes common initiatives like mindfulness and stress management for you, these targeted solutions fail to comprehensively address root systemic causes like the loss of your professional autonomy.

Your need for autonomy can ultimately be addressed in several ways, but in the end, it's important to understand that the current traditional employment system will not likely provide it.

MANY OPTIONS

There are so many iterations of how you can structure your professional life to provide you with your desired level of autonomy and control. This is not a one-size-fits-all concept. It's just the opposite. This is a journey towards self-defining what will best help you reach your goals while leveraging all of your earned assets, especially by activating your small business powers. Rethinking and reorganizing old ideas like professional corporations can often lead to a host of new opportunities worth exploring.

Most have been led to believe that there are only two primary options to work in the medical field: employment or private practice. This is a false dichotomy, and I will cover various job options in greater detail in Chapter 8 and explain how you can connect your PC to each one.

In my humble view, the PC-employment lite option provides the best of all worlds by operating under the less risky cover of employment. It also gives you the benefits of a small business and its associated greater professional control over your life.

SUMMARY

- Employment remains the best option for launching your career as an attending physician due to its many advantages.

- Once the honeymoon is over, you will experience some of the challenges of employment that ultimately erode your professional autonomy and thrust you towards burnout.

- You must make adaptive changes to thrive as an employed doctor, and starting your PC is the most important adaptation you can make.

CHAPTER 6

CORRECTIVE ACTION

WHEN I REACHED THE BREAKING POINT IN MY CAREER AND needed a change, I knew I had to take steps to identify the root cause of my problem and then implement a solution that corrected this cause to prevent its recurrence. Within organizations, this is called a corrective action plan.

There were several factors that I had to consider when making my plan for a future that addressed my root problem. First, my wife and I decided we did not want to move, having just built a custom home a few years earlier. Furthermore, I liked the benefits of employment and was willing to stay with the same employer if my conditions for change could be met.

I recognized that it would be much easier to take a new job with a new employer and start with a fresh slate to rebuild my professional life. In contrast, making the necessary tear down and then rebuilding it all while still working in the same job would be like remodeling the kitchen and bathroom in your house, all while living there. It's doable but inconvenient and challenging. However, my employer was willing to do it, so I pressed into exploring options that would allow me to circumvent the employee compensation ceiling while also allowing me to conform to the expected behaviors of their corporate citizens.

The key element to the entire remix was that I needed a professional infrastructure that allowed me greater control over my personal and professional life. The loss of autonomy was ultimately the root cause problem for me that needed a corrective action plan. As I had discovered in the prior decade, I could not depend on my employer to provide this for me. For them, the loss of my professional autonomy was inconsequential and did not need to be corrected.

INTERNAL INVENTORY

Up to this point, my entire identity was wrapped up in my life as a rural doctor who loved his family, faith community, and employer. My practice crisis forced me to finally pull my head up from my performance-based hard-charging nature, and look around to assess where I was in space. This involved asking other business professionals to help me take inventory, but it also involved a deeply personal holistic internal evaluation that included input from my wife. The reality was that although I highly valued my marriage and family life, my career aspirations and success were built upon my wife's broad shoulders. She made our complex blended family of five children soar. It wasn't that I wasn't involved, but like many medical marriages, she was left to do a lot of heavy lifting after we mutually made decisions about our personal lives.

Although it was functional, it added to the unseen metaphysical crisis of identity that was underneath my professional successes. My practice and financial successes also hid a lot of evolving issues that came crashing down due to the disillusionment I was now having with my trusted employer, whom I had loyally helped thrive.

On top of all this, the massive workload associated with the departures of the other doctors from my clinic was now becoming incredibly burdensome. The sum was that I could hear the hoofbeats of burnout drawing nearer, and I knew changes had to happen soon.

REORGANIZING MY PROFESSIONAL FUTURE

I determined that whoever employed me in my next step would need to provide staffing and practice management support that would have to be non-traditional and extend beyond what was considered normal staffing ratios due to my large patient panel size and heavy workload.

In addition to this, whoever employed me would need to reassure me that I would always be paid at a fair market value rate based on my productivity rather than be boxed in by some organizational formula.

I also determined that I needed a business team to help coach and guide me in the decision-making process associated with my professional life. In essence, I had reached the end of my rope with my self-sufficiency. I realized it had led me to the edge of burnout, and this juncture in my professional life needed to be a pivot to change how I organized both my personal and professional lives.

No longer could I rely exclusively on my employer to lead me to a better life; rather, I needed my team to work with me and look out for my best interests. This was a team that was disconnected from my employer and whose sole objective was to help me thrive personally and professionally.

So after completing my self-assessment in conjunction with my wife, I identified a group of consultants to help me formulate a remix of my employment via an action plan that would restore more of my professional autonomy. After hearing my story and understanding my personal and professional goals, this team then carefully helped identify the assets that I had assembled in the prior ten to fifteen years that were valuable to protect but could also be used as bargaining chips at the negotiation table.

I was aware of some of these assets, but others I was, frankly, ignorant of. Together they all added up to the awareness that I had a marketplace value that superseded my employer's view of my value. Due to this, I realized that I possessed a business power far greater than a typical non-physician employee.

KNOW YOUR VALUE

My team helped me evaluate my current professional state and the business assets, powers, and opportunities that were under my control. These then could all be used to help build my preferred future state. This was an interesting exercise because it revealed my unawareness of my true business value.

Unfortunately, I think this is a widespread experience for many employed doctors who have long given up a view of themselves as having marketplace business value and instead myopically focus on their compensation only. The following is what my consultants helped me discover through the eyes of a business professional in terms of what could and should be useful at the negotiation table with my employer:

1. **No Non-Compete**: My contract had been wisely shaped by my predecessor in the years before to NOT include a non-compete clause as part of my employment. It was grandfathered in with each contractual renewal. This was huge in terms of the opportunities it opened up, including contracting with any employer while allowing me to not have to move or commute to a new community. Now my employer knew I was aware that both my professional services AND my patient panel were open to the free market. In other words, they were now competing with other employers for my services and my large patient panel. This also provided me the opportunity to become independent because of my loyal and large patient panel. But private practice would also require a massive upfront cost associated with purchasing a medical office building, outfitting it, contracting with third parties, and re-recruiting my patients in a medical neighborhood nearly 100 percent aligned with my current employer. The start-up cost would require significant loans and, thus, a long-term commitment to stay in this market. This all made complete independence from my employer a risky and less desirable option for me.

2. **Market Share**: Healthcare employers want market share, and physicians are the tool for accessing their patient panels. Employers feign interest in doctors, but they want the three-fold revenue streams associated

with you and your patients. In essence, whoever controls the patients, controls the revenue. Point 1, above, helped me understand I still controlled the patients who would likely follow me to any employer and thus provide any employer a large market share. Therefore my employer was not just at risk of losing me but was at risk of losing a significant portion of their market share to any competing employer.

3. **Undervalued Compensation**: My Fair Market Value (FMV) compensation was just assumed by me in the context of my wRVU-based compensation model. I was wrong. Even before my employer tried to place a ceiling on my compensation, my consultant exposed the truth that my current compensation model was well below the MGMA market rate. When this discovery was added to my employer's plan to "cap" my compensation, it was even more insulting to my true value. In essence, I did not know my value. This is commonplace among doctors who choose to represent themself with employers and ultimately trust their employer in the fairness of their compensation package. This is one of many reasons you need an agent and agency to represent you so you can confirm your FMV. Learning my FMV allowed me to apply leverage when negotiating with my employer.

4. **Large Downstream Revenue**: The value of my downstream revenue to my employer ranged between $3–5 million. This ultimately was what any employer was after from me, pushing me to look at joint venture models that would capture lab, radiology, and ambulatory ancillary services within an employment agreement. However, due to multiple kickback regulations and antitrust rules,

a joint venture as an employed physician would not be a viable option for retaining this economic power. Even so, the knowledge that I created such enormous downstream revenue for my employer meant that I knew they desperately wanted to keep me employed.

5. **Real Estate**: Most employers prefer not to own brick-and-mortar clinical space but like to lease space for several business reasons. I determined that my employer was going to lease space from a third party for my clinical practice regardless of where I was located. My current state was that my practice site was paying a nonmedical real estate investor a large amount of money to lease the medical office building where I was located. This represented a business opportunity for me since my employer would pay for a fair market lease wherever I was located, and my future practice site did not have to be in the location that I was working in at that time.

6. **Small Business Power**: Although my powers had been dormant for years, my consultants helped me understand that I still owned this important asset and could be activated within the right conditions. Like most of you, I was led to believe that choosing employment meant I couldn't own my PC. I was wrong, as my consultants helped me discover. I could use my leverage with my employer at this exact moment to force them to allow me to transition from traditional employment to an employment model built upon my PC's activation.

With the help of consultants, I became aware of a hidden employment option called employment lite that would provide an architecture that would allow me to maximize all of the business powers, assets, and opportunities at my disposal. It would involve forming my own Professional Corporation (PC) and then wrapping a robust small business structure around it.

This would help restore my professional autonomy through the power of running my own small business while also providing the best structure to maximize my financial health and personal well-being. In addition, the employment lite model would result in my professional corporation becoming the intermediary between my employer and me yet still allow me to look much like a typical employee in their safe harbor.

Visually it looks like Figure 6.1.

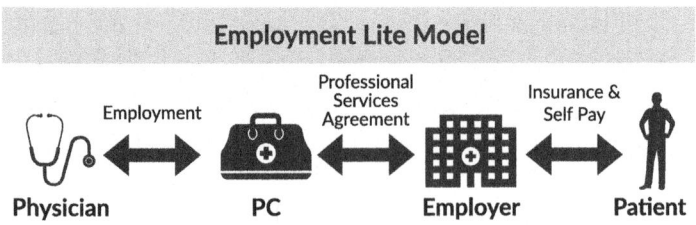

Figure 6.1

This is in contrast to my previous employment model, which looks like Figure 6.2.

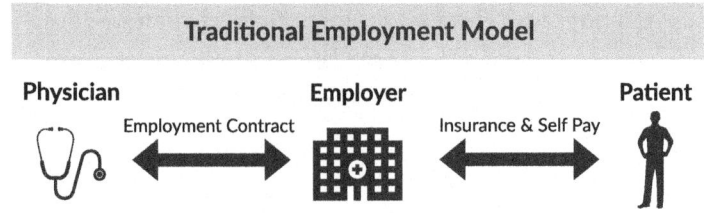

Figure 6.2

This novel PC-based employment model looked good on paper and showed some promise to be a corrective plan to help resolve the core cause of my crisis and prevent its future recurrence. However, I was a little unsure about starting my PC while being employed because it was so counter-intuitive. Thus, I asked my consultants for more evidence that it would work, especially in addressing one of my primary concerns about fair market compensation from my employer.

They carefully explained how small business owners possess autonomy and control over their professional and personal lives. Thus, starting my PC would help restore my fundamental need to regain some professional control in my life. Yet the PC-employment lite model would still allow me to hold onto the safety and security of working within my employer's harbor, shielded from the intense competition and management issues that private practices endure.

In regard to the compensation problem, they compared my compensation within traditional employment and contrasted it to receiving the same gross compensation through my PC. They were confident that a PC business structure would allow me to retain more of my income due to their experience operating their own small businesses. At this point, we were both aware that I deserved to be paid more by my employer, but we wanted to assume the worst-case scenario in our "what if" evaluation. Therefore, the key variable of my capped compensation would be the same when contrasting the PC-employment lite structure with my current employment. Figure 6.3 reveals this case study.

Case Study

Traditional Employment Doctor as Hospital Employee		Employment Lite Employed Doctor as PC with PSA	
W-2 Employee		1099 & W-2 Employee	
Financial Structure Pay + Benefits Paid by Employer		**Financial Structure** Pay + Benefits Paid by PC	
Gross Pay to Doctor	$421,000	Gross Pay to Doctor	$422,000
Professional Overhead & Expenses (CME, Malpractice, etc.)	$23,857	Professional Overhead & Expenses (Business Expenses, CME, Malpractice, etc.)	$38,857
Healthcare Provided by Hospital	$30,143	Healthcare Provided by PC	$24,000

All federal, state, social security, Medicare, and local taxes have been stripped out here

Household Money		Household Money	
Net Paycheck Annually	$214,000	Net Paycheck from PC Annually	$150,000
Tax-Deferred Retirement Plans	$35,500	Business Distributions Annually	$25,000
		Tax-Advantaged Income Home	$24,000
		Tax-Deferred Retirement Plans with PC	$97,000

Net Economic Benefit to Doctor Household	Net Economic Benefit to Doctor Household
$249,900	$320,000

Net Income Retained	
Annually	$70,500
5 Years	$352,500
10 Years	$705,000

Figure 6.3

Structuring my PC in this comparison involved using the SimpliMD small business model, which we'll discuss further in Chapter 9. Here are the highlights of the side-by-side comparison of my traditional employment versus the new PC-based employment lite architecture:

1. **Compensation (Gross Pay to Doctor)**: I would receive the same pay from the employer regardless of whether I received it personally or via my PC. This was an important starting point because their one non-negotiable feature was that they could not pay me more as an employee. Thus my case study had to start with this premise.

2. **Professional Overhead and Expenses**: This includes CME, professional society membership, malpractice, life and disability insurance, and licensing fees. In traditional employment, these were paid by my employer and could be a combination of both untaxed and taxed fringe benefits. Within employment lite, these were now the sole responsibility of my PC but now became untaxed business expenses that flowed through my company.

3. **Healthcare Expenses**: This benefit, including health, dental, and eye insurance, was covered as an untaxed benefit from my employer. Within employment lite, your PC covers the cost of this as a business expense. In my case, I was able to join a health plan that was much cheaper than my employer's plan. Sourcing your own benefits seemed like a huge hill to climb, but it turns out to be easily outsourced. Additionally, when your benefits are placed under your control, they can be crafted to best benefit your entire household.

4. **Household Money**: Within PC-employment lite, this component requires you to shift your understanding of how the money arrives in your home. Your "take-home" pay in traditional employment is pretty straightforward after taxes and retirement plans are paid. However, in the PC business structure, you will pay yourself W-2 income as an owner-employee, and you can also consider hiring your spouse within the company as another source of household income. In my case, my wife was hired as the corporate bookkeeper. As I will explain later, your business structure will create additional income channels, and thus, all your income no longer has to come from your paycheck. This, in turn, will allow you to be paid less, resulting in you paying fewer taxes on your W-2 earned income from your PC. As you can see in the case study, our actual pay from the PC would be much less than it was from my hospital employer. This smaller paycheck made me nervous because I was so used to getting a simple large deposit from my employer every few weeks. Since I didn't understand how small businesses operated at this point, I hesitated to do this despite the reassurance of my business consultants. It took about a year before I fully understood this secret sauce of how a small business structure and the actual cash flow ultimately benefited my household.

5. **Income Channels**: A key concept for small businesses is that your paycheck is just one element of how money ultimately lands in your household. Beyond earned income as an employee of your PC, the other elements include business distributions,

tax-advantaged income to the home, and tax-deferred retirement plans. Note how these are all line items on the employment lite side only. I will explain each in more detail in Chapters 7 and 9; note all four of these channels will flow out of your 1099 income generated by your PC. These extra channels provide resources that benefit your household and grow your net worth faster, mainly due to the more robust retirement savings. But the flow of those total dollars into your bank account will be more asynchronous than the singular bank deposit you are used to. This does take a bit to get used to. In comparison, traditional employment only provides one channel, your earned income. Due to your high income, the tax drag on your earnings makes it more disadvantaged to grow your household net worth solely through this channel.

6. **Retained Income**: This is the result of this business model. It represents the amount of money I could hold onto, or retain, through the power of wise business structuring and tax-advantaged strategies that are available primarily to small businesses. I could now receive the same pay from my employer, and keep $70,000 more than I had under traditional W-2 employment. This does not mean that W-2 employees don't have the opportunity to retain income through itemized tax deductions like charitable contributions and tax-advantaged retirement plans. But for those with high income, like physicians, the number of options is shrinking. By adding in the power of small business tax advantages, you can significantly multiply your tax strategy options. I cover more details on this in Chapter 9.

THE FINANCIAL BENEFITS OF PC-EMPLOYMENT LITE

In summary, this case study proved that for the same compensation, a new business architecture would lower my monthly paycheck but would paradoxically provide me with more household income, give me more control over my life, and allow me to grow my net worth faster.

Even if I didn't change anything in regard to my employer's compensation formula, changes on my end alone would lead to significant financial benefits to my household annually. This was HUGE because it affirmed my perception that my professional services were worth more than was landing in my household. It also proved that I could increase my household income without working harder or longer. Once I had this established, I could circle back to the other conditions that I felt were critical to my long-term personal and professional satisfaction.

After confirming that my best employment structure for the rebuilding process was PC-employment lite, I began to consider the other professional practice changes needed within the business and the non-business elements. I knew I had to address solutions that would make my work-home balance more sustainable, as well as better control the growing burden of my uncompensated corporate citizenship duties.

THE PSYCHOLOGICAL BENEFITS OF PC-EMPLOYMENT LITE

During my internal inventory, I realized that the loss of my personal and professional autonomy was one of the most important underlying forces causing me moral harm. Thus, any restart of my professional life had to swing the professional autonomy pendulum back toward a healthier balance.

The PC-employment lite structure provided the needed antidote for this because it empowered me to organize and monetize my professional services via side jobs that I had previously done for free as a good corporate citizen. I gave up my corporate governance roles due to the big-time commitments and negotiated compensation for call, sideline sports medicine coverage, and extender oversight.

In addition to this, I accepted an assistant medical director role with a local nursing home. Somehow psychologically gaining control over "having to do things" versus "choosing to do things" made a big difference.

On top of that, it felt good to get paid for things I had been doing for free. This reinforced my PC's power to add income channels to my small business and home. The light bulb began to come on—I could act like a small business and use my professional services to diversify my revenue sources beyond more than one source. The net benefit, psychologically and financially, was very positive.

WORK-HOME CONDITIONS

Outside of the clinic, I was spending a lot of time at the hospital providing acute care to a wide range of patients. The call and coverage for this created an unpredictable day-to-day clinical life for me that was uncontrollable and disrupted my clinic and home life.

As I reorganized things, I prioritized my long-standing passion for obstetrics and newborn care (I have completed an FP-OB Fellowship) and gave up adult inpatient care. I also determined the fair market compensation for continuing to take call for unassigned hospital patients and included this in my list of needed changes. This monetization of the call would allow me to easily assess its value in connection to its time commitment. In other words, it was now a personal business decision, not a corporate citizen requirement.

In the clinic, I wanted to increase control of my future and thus volunteered to pilot a patient-centered medical home model at a new clinical location (that I would own and rent to my employer) where I would supervise multiple team members, including NPs, a pharmacist, and RNs who would help deliver holistic care. I instituted an EHR solution by adopting the TeamCare model of having three nurse-scribes work directly with me in delivering direct patient care. Thus I could see more patients efficiently but also not do any EHR work at home, all while ensuring I got home nightly between 5:00 and 6:00 p.m.

I also wanted a three-day weekend along with a four-day workweek to have more space for recovery from work. So I created a schedule that allowed me to take Mondays off while my NPs covered the clinic.

All of this added up to the necessary conditions that my employer would have to support for me to continue working for them.

NEGOTIATIONS

After creating the key elements of my employment remix, I was prepared to negotiate with my employer about the conditions needed to retain my professional services.

So I shot for the moon and got all that I wanted because my employer was in a highly vulnerable position of potentially losing a large percentage of their market share as well as a highly productive physician.

The fundamental components of my ideal professional life included each of the following elements. I believed each of these would give me a greater sense of control over my professional life and my financial future.

- **EHR solutions via TeamCare Medicine-Scribes +**

- **PC-Employment Lite Contract +**

- **SimpliMD small business model**

ADDITIONAL VALUE OPPORTUNITIES

During this time, after the basic structure of the new deal was agreed upon that included all the items mentioned above, then two important elements were additionally negotiated to be connected to it.

The first was a provision to purchase a medical office building and move my practice to that location with my employer promising to pay a long-term fair market lease for that space. They agreed to this, and I quickly capitalized by purchasing a suitable commercial building, converting it to a medical office building, and then locked in a lease with them.

The second was evaluating whether I was being compensated at a fair market value for my professional services, hospital call, and medical leadership. Again, my mantra was not to do more work but to get paid for the work I was currently doing.

My conversion to the PC-employment lite contract helped me because it allowed both parties to create a compensation model that was outside their standard employment contract, which had a cap on the maximum compensation. This was possible because, technically, I was now considered an independent contractor rather than an employee, and their compensation formula could only be legally enforced with their employees. Thus they could provide my PC with a fair market independent contractor salary or productivity formula rather than a standard employee compensation formula.

We agreed to use MGMA-based metrics at a per wRVU rate to arrive at fair compensation. The hospital call, medical leadership, and other professional services were negotiated to a fair compensation rate for both parties. In the end, due to the lagging compensation model from my employer, I received a significant income raise for all that I was doing.

PC-Employee Lite Conversion
Financial Downstream

Annual Value	
SimpliMD Model Retained Income	$70,500
Fair Market Value Increase in Pre-tax Compensation	$147,000
Total:	$217,500
Ten-Year Value	
Total:	$2,175,000*

*Pre-tax

Figure 6.4

This is laid out in Figure 6.4. It is not a typo, nor is it a hypothetical case. Instead, this transition to PC-employment lite would provide me with this extra income (on top of my regular earnings) over the next ten years. Incredibly it did not require any additional work on my part, but rather fit into the important mindset of "working smarter, not harder." My PC-employment lite structure allowed me to add over $200,000 per year to my household via a combination of retained income and fair market value pre-tax income.

And the icing on the cake was I now was leasing my own medical office building to my employer, had a four-day work week, had a three-day weekend, had three scribe-nurses, and could do CME (paid by my PC) anywhere in the world that I wanted.

All of this was made possible by simply choosing to wisely organize around my earned assets which included tapping into my small business superpower. Please note that this does not mean you would have the same results if you followed my lead, but I can tell you that you are losing out on a lot of money by not understanding how you can use all of the assets you have earned.

This is a powerful story because it simultaneously provides a roadmap to recover from burnout as well as prevent future burnout via its empowerment of professional autonomy. Additionally, it helps you retain more of your hard-earned income, which hastens your arrival to Stage 3 of your career. The combination of these two elements means your household's net worth is growing without you having to work harder or longer all while your well-being is fortified.

SUMMARY

- PC-employment lite is a novel employment model that can help you recover from burnout and has the potential to help prevent burnout due to its restoration of your professional autonomy.

- You should enlist other professionals to help you understand the value of your earned assets in the marketplace.

- PC-employment lite is a market correction to physician employment that can increase your professional autonomy and improve your household financial position and personal well-being.

CHAPTER 7

ONE SIMPLE CHANGE

PC.

Adding these two letters to the end of your name is simplistic on one hand, but most importantly, it signals your empowerment to see yourself as a business. Unlike MD and DO, which identify your professional degree as an individual, these two letters, PC, communicate a different message about you. You are a business.

The empowerment and resolve to use your small business power could ignite a significant movement that changes the current system of employment and will provide alternative job structure options like PC-employment lite that better support your well-being.

The catalyst for this important paradigm shift is the addition of these two simple letters to your name.

DISRUPTION OF THE STATUS QUO

Disruptive change occurs when the fundamental concepts and processes of business patterns start to quickly shift. While small incremental changes allow employees to adapt slowly over time, disruptive changes to work systems can cause a rapid shift to a new way of life. Large corporations often prefer incremental changes because they are less risky.

In the context of physician employment, incremental changes would include things like adjusting compensation formulas, progressive staffing models such as scribes or the use of extenders, resiliency training, and EHRs that reduce physician workload. All of these improvements make work more sustainable for doctors. They are valuable and important elements associated with making employed doctors' lives better.

Disruptive change, on the other hand, occurs when business models are fundamentally challenged, changed, and (re)invented. This would involve making systemic changes that alter the current model of traditional employment and the way employers and employees interface.

Most would agree that systemic changes are needed within physician employment, but employers are often too concerned with the risks of disruption to their operations from these changes. Therefore, they would prefer to adopt less risky incremental changes.

The trigger for large corporations to adopt disruptive changes is often brought on by disruptive innovation. In essence, innovation forces the abandonment of incremental change in favor of disruptive change because the risk of losing market share for large corporations is larger than the risks of making changes.

An excellent example of a market leader faltering because it chose incremental change over disruptive changes is Eastman Kodak. It is an iconic example of a company that failed to grasp the significance of a needed transition that threatened its business. After decades of being an undisputed world leader in film photography, Kodak couldn't see the fundamental shift from analog to digital technology that was happening right under its nose. Their sluggish response ultimately led to their demise and bankruptcy.

Disruptive innovation within healthcare employment is needed so that it will trigger a rapid adaptive change by employers to respond to the innovation. The failure to adapt to it must be sufficiently threatening to their business model that, much like Kodak, the marketplace will leave them behind if they don't adapt.

Physicians as a whole, but particularly young doctors, have the power to cause this type of disruptive innovation through the formation of the modern micro-PC that is then linked to a novel employment model, such as employment lite. Forcing employers to deal with physicians as a PC would disrupt the current status quo system of employment. It would return physicians to a greater position of control over their professional life and change what physician employees expect from their employers and vice versa.

In turn, this would lead employers to embrace this change or risk losing the physician recruitment and retention competition to their corporate foes. Given the aforementioned growing physician shortage, competitive advantages and creative adaptations are necessary for healthcare corporations to maintain and grow their market share.

Thus, they would need to adjust to this market change or lose out in the competition for your professional services. The overall demand for your services gives you the upper hand in this process, and the more competition for you, the more power you have to define the business relationship. In general, you will find the early adopters of these changes will be smaller or rural employers because flexibility is one of their marketplace advantages.

Given the current burnout crisis for physicians, both incremental and disruptive changes are needed for our profession. PC-employment lite offers a simple and powerful change to the current state of employment that is both incremental and disruptive.

I believe the best feature of this systemic change is that while it does change things, it is subtle enough not to significantly disrupt either party. The most powerful piece is that it is a systemic change that allows physicians to stay aligned within an employer's safe harbor, but simultaneously restores their professional and personal autonomy.

THE LESS DISRUPTIVE CHANGE

Deep down inside, I think you recognize the need for adaptive changes to your professional life that will allow you to thrive in a system that can be harmful to you. But what you fear is choosing an adaptive path that is too disruptive to the professional life that you have finally been able to reach in Stage 2 of your life.

You don't want a massive change that will negatively impact your family life and lifestyle. The constant changes for you and your loved ones that are connected to your training process make you long for stability and predictability. Thus, choosing employment is wise due to the way it meets these needs.

With this in mind, the innovative idea of forming your own PC within today's marketplace seems to carry a great deal of disruptive risk to your life. Yes, it's an adaptive opportunity for you, but when you look at your existing business model of employment, you hear Mark Twain's famous refrain echo through your brain, "Every once in a while one stumbles across a good idea, but with any luck, you'll right yourself and pass it by." Thus as you read this book and understand how the innovation of starting your own micro-PC coupled with employment lite can benefit you, you will be tempted to walk away from it due to fear over its feasibility.

However, one of the things that makes this adaptive change so profound is that while it is an innovative business model, it is actually a minimally disruptive marketplace solution for your professional life. That is because it allows you to remain employed in every beneficial aspect that is considered traditional yet provides you with greater control over your personal and professional life through the operation of your own small business micro-PC. You don't have to move, change employers, or negotiate a complicated new contract.

Your only disruption is that you have to shift your mindset, and then add two simple letters to your name on your employment contract. "Dr. You, **PC**" makes all the difference. It can be simple and uncomplicated for both you and your employer.

A traditional contract and an employment lite contract are essentially the same other than the "who" that is listed in the agreement.

PURCHASED SERVICES

To your employer, a PC-employment lite contractual change will shift how they view you professionally and financially. Now your employment expenses are tracked within their finance department as "purchased services" rather than as "physician employment."

Purchased services generically are a labor expense category for companies and are most commonly associated with hiring independent contractors to supply professional services from any healthcare specialty or service line.

Traditionally this has been associated with the high costs for locum tenens or the expenses related to acute care service lines such as ER doctors, hospitalists, or anesthesia. But in today's world, these purchased services don't only apply to doctors but also to travel nurses, therapists, and virtually every flavor of healthcare employee you can imagine.

When your employer purchases these professional services, they will cover agreed-upon compensation expenses and agency fees, provide no benefits, and typically collect all the billable services based upon the contractual agreement.

Overall, this space of purchased services costs employers more money for the same professional services compared to traditional employees. As I will explain in Chapter 10 on the gatekeepers, the general higher cost of purchased services will make many employers worry that a PC-employment lite agreement will be more expensive than traditional employment. The fact is that this is not true. Unlike locums physicians, there are no agency expenses involved with employment lite. The compensation rate for PC-employment lite is typically much less than the higher rates needed to pay for locums coverage, particularly because there are no agency fees involved.

The specific terms of these professional service agreements can vary, as can their fair market value. Professional service agreements (PSA, like PC-employment lite) are business-to-business relationship contracts through which an employer purchases your professional services.

It's not unusual to bring up the subject of PC-employment lite to an employer and have them respond with a simplistic, "We don't do that with our employed doctors," because they fear the higher labor expense associated with professional service agreements.

Your response should be, "But you do purchase professional services with other doctors, and I would like to offer you a less expensive version of this. The PC-employment lite structure can even reduce your labor expenses to less than your traditional employee."

Your PC-employment lite contract will provide them with your professional services in a highly aligned manner, but lead to many personal benefits for you on the backside. This arrangement will help you save them money in comparison to traditional employees because they will shed the expenses associated with your benefits package as well as payroll taxes. On top of this, they will still maintain their control over your specialty-driven professional services.

In my opinion, PC-employment lite should be categorized by the finance department as a subset of physician employee expenses on the corporate spreadsheet, rather than purchased services. This is because you will act much more like an employee than a locum and your true labor expense is less than any of the other professional service models.

This may be semantics, but CFOs and CEOs tend to view employees with fondness and purchased or contracted services as a problem to resolve. Thus campaigning to make you a subset of the highly aligned and more economical employment expenses will increase the likelihood of this innovative model being embraced and supported.

For example, my employer is a very large national healthcare company and due to their ten-figure loss sustained during the COVID pandemic, they had to make massive spending cuts in many categories, ranging from real estate to staffing to labor costs. The labor expense that was easiest for them to target was eliminating purchased services at all levels. While this is a sensible decision, it fails to take into account the small number of physicians like myself who are technically purchased professional services but who act like traditional employees. No worries by the way, I didn't lose my job, but I did have to painstakingly explain to the C-suite why I was different from their other purchased services.

THE PURCHASED SERVICES AGREEMENT

PC-employment lite is a type of Purchased Service Agreement (PSA) because it represents professional medical services purchased by your employer from a vendor (PC) outside of their healthcare system. Historically these services provided by contractors can be complicated in terms of defining the scope of work involved.

In contrast, a PSA for your specialty-driven professional services through your PC is not very complicated because it will mirror the same scope of work as your fellow traditional employees. In regard to your employer, transitioning you from your traditional employment agreement to an employment lite agreement simply involves using virtually the same traditional contract and adding PC to your name in the agreement. That's it, that's all.

PURCHASED SERVICES AGREEMENT

This Purchased Services Agreement ("Agreement") is entered into by and between ▮▮▮▮ Network, ("Corporation") and Tod A. Stillson M.D., P.C. ("Provider") for the services of Tod Stillson, M.D. (referred to as "Physician").

I. PHYSICIAN DUTIES

    A. Provider, through Physician, shall provide professional primary care physician services to patients at ▮▮▮▮▮▮▮▮▮▮▮▮▮▮▮▮▮▮, devoting a minimum of 40 hours per week to the practice of medicine of which a minimum of 36 hours per week shall be devoted to scheduled patient visits ▮▮▮▮ and Physician shall be available to act as a collaborating physician for Corporation's nurse practitioners as needed ("Primary Care Services").

    B. Provider, through Physician, shall provide PRN professional medical services as an unrestricted, on-call ▮▮▮▮▮▮▮▮▮▮▮▮▮▮ at those times mutual agreed upon by Corporation and Physician; generally between the hours of 7:00 P.M. and 7:00 A.M. ("PRN Hospitalist Services").

Figure 7.1

Now their HR department will no longer take anything out of your paycheck and will switch their IRS reporting designation to 1099 which means you will be given the full control and responsibility to manage the flow of your income through all of your fiduciary obligations, like taxes and any desired benefits.

As you can see in the copy of my contract reproduced in Figure 7.1, the agreement is between the employer and your PC and is further designated as the services that you personally provide.

Like any contract, the PSA will outline your duties as a physician, compensation, the employer's duties, and other elements common to any standard employment agreement. For a more complete breakdown of PSAs, take a look at the Coker Group's white paper on them that is found online.

The focus of your conversation with your employer should be about your professional services and how they are aligned with their organization. Whether they receive these services from you within a business structure or as an individual should not matter to them, nor is it really their prerogative. Either way, they are contractually purchasing your professional work.

As long as the contractual services are met at the same fair market compensation as their employees, why should it matter to them which entity provides it? Employers often overlook the fact that professionally you are both a business and an individual, and thus either entity can deliver the desired services. You may have to remind them that you have earned this option, but you may also have to remind yourself that you have earned this special small business power, and it's fully up to you whether or not to unlock it.

This one simple change—to add PC to the end of your name—puts in motion a cascade of outcomes that all add up to making your life better through the use of one of your most important earned assets, your small business superpower. Let's take a look at these benefits and consider whether this would be worth pursuing for your career and medical life.

A SYSTEMIC BURNOUT SOLUTION

The current traditional employment model that involves yielding all of your professional powers to a large corporation has created an alarming burnout rate for our profession. The association between the system of traditional employment and burnout is clear and flies in the face of employment being a safe space for you to live your professional life. Although employers do provide some benevolent protection from the highly volatile healthcare economy in their so-called safe harbor, this model fails to take into consideration the slow but catastrophic effects of the loss of professional autonomy that happen to you in this space.

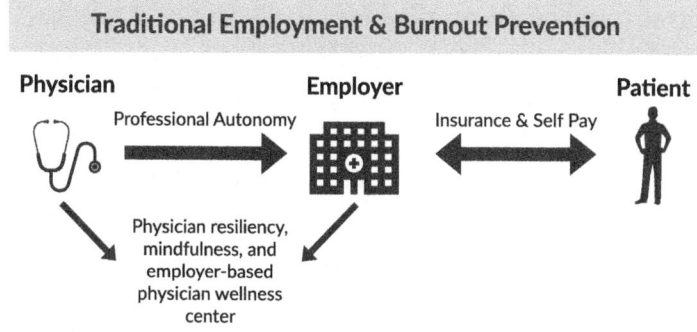

Figure 7.2

Too many doctors are being injured in the current system that makes them feel co-dependently trapped in it, which is further intensified by employers whose primary solution to this tension is to provide physician resiliency programs, as illustrated in Figure 7.2. Although this is helpful for you, it falls short of addressing any causative systemic issues. As employers and physicians search for solutions to help prevent your burnout, this innovative employment change provides real solutions to the systemic causes, all while keeping you operating within the space of your employer's safe harbor. This change simultaneously returns some of the control to your personal and professional life. When control and autonomy are returned to your life, it dramatically improves your well-being, making you happier and more satisfied.

The idea that changing the system leads to a greater sense of well-being has been affirmed in the literature, where having primary control or mastery of your circumstances is most commonly associated with the "good life."[64] You might wonder, *How does a sense of control relate to well-being?* To fully understand this, you must consider two distinguishable control strategies that humans deploy when they are distressed. One is primary control and the other is secondary control. These two control strategies have different relationships with subjective well-being, daily positive or negative affective experiences, and global life satisfaction.

Primary control refers to behaviors directed at the external environment and involves attempts to change them in order to meet the needs of the individual. Secondary control is targeted

---

64 Erik G. Helzer and Eranda Jayawickreme, "Control and the 'Good Life': Primary and Secondary Control as Distinct Indicators of Well-Being," *Social Psychological and Personality Science* 6, no. 6 (2015): 653–660, https://doi.org/10.1177/1948550615576210.

at internal processes and serves to minimize losses in, maintain, and expand existing levels of primary control.

Secondary control strategies involve the person manipulating their internal cognitive/affective states in order to reduce the psychological impact of events. This is the realm of interpersonal resiliency and mindfulness programs that have been universally embraced as a solution by all.

These secondary control measures are valuable but don't turn out to be nearly as valuable to physicians as primary control measures that address the systemic causes of their distress. Primary control adaptations are more highly connected to improved subjective well-being as well as global life satisfaction. PC-employment lite offers a primary control option for doctors due to the way it increases the control of your personal and professional life.

PROFESSIONAL BENEFITS

When I transitioned to this better employment model, in many regards, not much changed in terms of the professional services that I provided to my community. I worked at the same clinic, used the same name tag, wore the same corporate brand, and pretty much blended in with the rest of my physician and non-physician associates.

Honestly, from the outside, no one could tell it happened, and that was my preference. I wanted to make it an invisible transition and continue to appear as though I was just another physician corporate citizen. But deep down inside, I now knew who

I worked for, and it was my own small business. Don't get me wrong, I still wanted my employer to be successful through my services. Their success through my professional services made us both business winners.

But this subtle and relatively invisible change did transform my mindset. I now felt empowered to place an economic and contractual value on each of my professional services, which psychologically resulted in me valuing myself more. My small business had power, and therefore, I had power.

As an example, let me discuss my obstetrical services that were highly important to my professional satisfaction. I had frequently requested that my employer advertise and communicate to our community that I was an obstetrical provider option for those seeking maternity care at our small rural hospital. The problem was that they also employed an OB-GYN and midwife and felt obligated to promote them through all their marketing channels.

Obstetrics was market share that they totally controlled, thus, marketing dollars spent on me personally would have little to no net revenue benefits to them because they would collect the system money for obstetrics regardless of who delivered the baby. In addition to that, their fiduciary alignment needed to be with the OB specialist who drove market share rather than a family doctor who did one-third of the OB's volume.

Highlighting my professional skills and interests to the public was viewed as unnecessary competition within their obstetrical service line. Thus my employer's website listing for me included OB care, but it was buried within the fine print only.

This was a bit frustrating since I am very tuned into the continuous need to inform young women that family doctors still provide maternity care.

On top of this, my employer's marketing department forbade employed doctors to form their own website or have social media presence because they demanded full digital control over their employees. Everything had to be approved and filtered by them. But when I formed my PC, I was emancipated from their full control (although there were still some corporate restrictions), and I could now create my own company's website and social media channels that would highlight my marketplace distinction—family practice-based surgical obstetrical services.

I had completed a fellowship in surgical obstetrics, and this was a unique earned asset that I wanted to be central to my practice. Although the website was a small thing, it signaled that I was now able to control and influence my space in my region's obstetrical market (Figure 7.3).

Figure 7.3

Constructed properly, it was outside of the reach of my employer's marketing department and brand management. Making myself a marketplace option via my digital presence was fundamental to any woman's phone search for an OB doctor.

Honestly, this was tremendously so empowering to me professionally because it allowed me to have a greater sense of autonomy over my obstetrical practice. It also allowed me to proactively fill my patient panel with the patient demographics that I preferred, which was young families.

Employment Benefits of Employment Lite

Much like traditional employment, PC-employment lite contracts provide you with the safety of working within your employer's harbor. Because you are still located in their safe harbor, you can confidently know that you are compliant with all federal and state professional service regulations.

Additionally, you will not have to manage or operate your medical practice because your employer provides all staff, management, clinic space, and equipment for you.

You are not subject to the financial risks associated with the constantly changing third-party reimbursement programs. Instead, your employer handles the billing and collections while paying you either a predictable salary or an agreed-upon compensation formula that is typically based on wRVUs.

Economic Benefits of Employment Lite

The predictable paycheck from your PC is a very nice feature of PC-employment lite, but it is not the only economic benefit.

Your PC provides you the power to control multiple fiduciary components of your personal and professional life that are uniquely fused in the micro-PC structure. Those include increased control of your taxes, benefits, household cash flow, retained income, and other income sources. Within your small business, you now gain full control of the flow of the dollars that you earn.

Figure 7.4 provides a broad view of how the business structure of your PC in connection with an employment lite contract benefits you by restoring your control of the dollars within your professional and personal financial state.

CONTROL OVER YOUR CASH FLOW

When you are able to receive your earnings from your corporate employer through your business first, you get to determine how each of your hard-earned dollars is used to benefit your household via a series of filters that include taxes. One of the secrets to increasing your household income and net worth is NOT by making more money, rather, it is by wise cash flow structures that allow you to retain more of what you have earned.

This flow chart in Figure 7.4 depicts a generalized view of the different taxation channels and business options unlocked by transitioning from a traditional employee agreement to a PC-employee lite agreement.

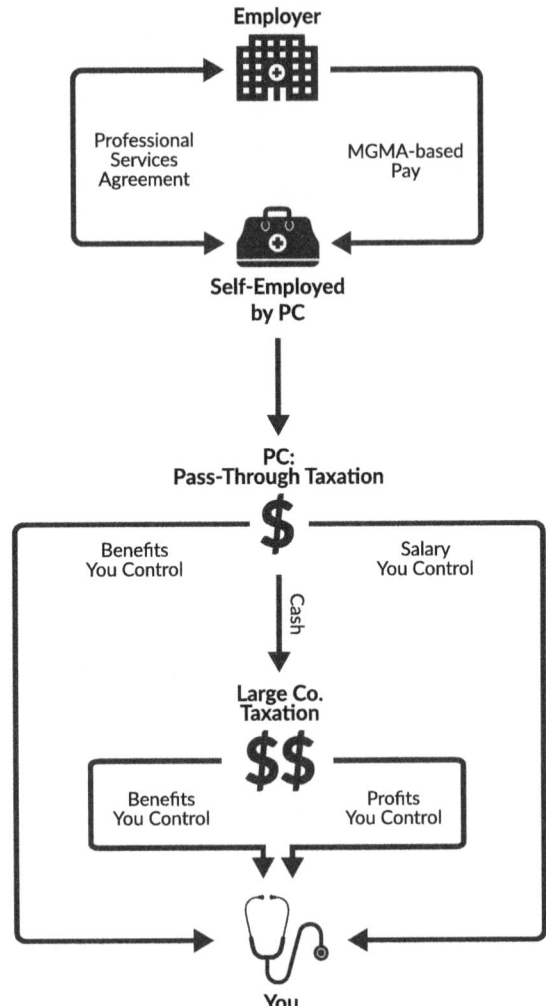

Figure 7.4

Different channels of cash flow have different taxation rules, with PCs typically electing S-Corp status and large companies electing C-Corp status.[65] S-Corps are considered pass-through taxation because the entity does not pay the taxes, rather, the income passes through to the owner, who pays personal income tax on their share. C-Corps, on the other hand, are taxed as an entity and then pay its shareholders dividends from its after-tax profits. The shareholders then pay personal income taxes on these dividends. This is the often-mentioned "double taxation."

By working with business and tax professionals, you can determine which business structure will work best to maximize your tax advantages, income, and benefits associated with each cash flow channel. Most of you will operate your micro-PC as an S-Corp and not include a C-Corp. But this can vary based on the size of your business income as well as the number of business interests and assets that make up your complete financial architecture. For instance, I use all three of these tax entities (individual, S-Corp, and C-Corp) to flow the income associated with my enterprise model. In Chapters 8 and 9, I will go into greater depth regarding all of this information.

The bottom line is that a PC-employment lite structure allows you to have the greatest control over your earned income. In turn, this places you in the best position to retain more of your earnings, which leads to the growth of your net worth and a more rapid arrival to financial independence.

---

65 "Business Types 101," LegalZoom, accessed November 27, 2022, https://www.legalzoom.com/business/business-formation/compare.html.

CONTROL OVER THE SOURCES OF INCOME THAT BENEFIT YOUR HOUSEHOLD

As I explained in my case study in Chapter 6, your self-employed W-2 income will be less in this small business model in comparison to the traditional employment model. Before you become concerned that you will have less money in your home due to a lower W-2 salary paid to you by your PC, let me refer you to Figure 7.5.

Individual	Household Income Source with PC
Individual	W-2 Paycheck to Doctor & Spouse
	+
PC	Business Distributions
	+
PC	Tax-Advantaged Household Income
	+
PC	Tax-Deferred Retirement Plan

Figure 7.5

You need to understand that your household income in this business model does not exclusively come from your personal W-2 income. Ultimately, the flow of money into your household will now come through multiple tax-advantaged channels that flow through your PC. This is a very common small business model and is all part of the original intent of the development of PCs many years ago.

Through this small business structure, your household net worth will grow faster as it flows to you through a combination of wages, untaxed benefits, business deductions, business distributions, and pre-tax retirement funding. This architecture reduces the tax burden related to your individual W-2 income through your PC, and the result is a lower effective tax rate on your household.

Through these IRS-compliant personal and small business tax strategies, I have been able to reduce both my total taxes paid and my effective tax rate compared to when I was a traditionally employed physician.

The simple addition of a PC to your name in connection with the contractual change to employment lite will unlock numerous personal and professional benefits that are not accessible to you as a traditional employee. The next chapter will expound more on the PC component of this employment model.

SUMMARY

- The directive for young doctors to start their micro-PC while in the latter stages of their training can become the catalyst to begin a national movement to help restore physician autonomy and prevent burnout.

- PC-employment lite provides a systemic solution to the broken status quo of traditional employment. It is a change that turns out to be the least disruptive to you and your employer.

- Although purchased services are typically a more expensive labor expense for employers, PC-employment lite is a special exception to this rule and will often cost employers less than their traditional employees.

- Your professional services are the fundamental interests of your employer, and the PC-employment lite model is the lowest cost option for them to acquire those services.

- A PC with employment lite provides you with greater control over your income, benefits, and professional life in comparison to traditional employment.

CHAPTER 8

WHAT'S OLD IS NEW

EACH BUSINESS COMPONENT OF THIS NEW VERSION OF A PC IS freely available within the public domain and can be commonly sourced. But ultimately, it's how the components are assembled in a modern business architecture that makes all the difference. This is not the same entity as the old private practice PC since the nuances of its business structure and function are much different than its evolved new edition. Thus it is very important not to assume that every PC structure is the same and to recognize that it is not a one-size-fits-all concept.

To understand that your modern micro-PC can be vastly different from its older version, let's look at the cell phone as an example. In 2007, Apple created the iPhone as an individualized handheld device for phone, text, email, internet access, calendars, and personalized apps. This highly efficient configuration of hardware and software in a very individualized system is what makes it so special. Although iPhones are ubiquitous, it's their personalized setup that makes everyone's iPhone unique, and thus special. No two are the same.

When I speak about PC-employment lite, I am referring to it much like I would an iPhone—generically, as a delivery platform or business system. This highly efficient configuration of the business, legal, tax, benefits, and retirement structures within it must be set up with the modern physician in mind and should be a highly individualized process. Ultimately, like iPhones, no two PC-employment lite structures are exactly alike because each one is a highly personalized entity.

There is an efficiency gained when the micro-PC business structure is created in a doctor-centric manner, but ultimately the purpose, identity, and personality of its design are unique to you. Just like your phone is similar, but different from everyone else's—so will your PC be similar but different from others'.

HOW PCS FIT INTO COMMON JOB STRUCTURES

To better understand the past, but also peer into the future, let's take a look at the current landscape of PCs and how they fit into the more common job structures that physicians work within today. This will allow us to disentangle PCs from each model while simultaneously looking at the "+ this" elements associated with each job structure.

Traditional Employment

Here you do not need a PC because your professional services are nearly 100 percent aligned with your employer. Although technically, if you are traditionally employed, you can form a micro-PC to manage your professional side jobs, most doctors don't. Many prefer the simplicity of flowing all of their individual taxpayer earnings through this structure. We discussed the many benefits of the traditional employment structure in Chapter 5. In this model, you essentially turn over your small business power to your employer and let them manage everything, including managing you. You should be mindful that this latter part does have some long-term implications due to its impact on your personal and professional autonomy.

Generally, this is how a PC fits into this employment model:

Traditional Employment = No PC*

*PCs are possible for traditional employees

Employment Lite

This model simply adds your micro-PC to your employment structure. It involves activating and operating your small business power through a PC. It provides you with greater control over your professional life since your professional services are no longer solely aligned with your employer (based on your contractual terms).

This model provides you greater control over your life due to the many known benefits of operating a small business, including greater control over your earned income. Ultimately, this is a hybrid version of employment and independent contracting. The structure looks like this in Figure 8.1.

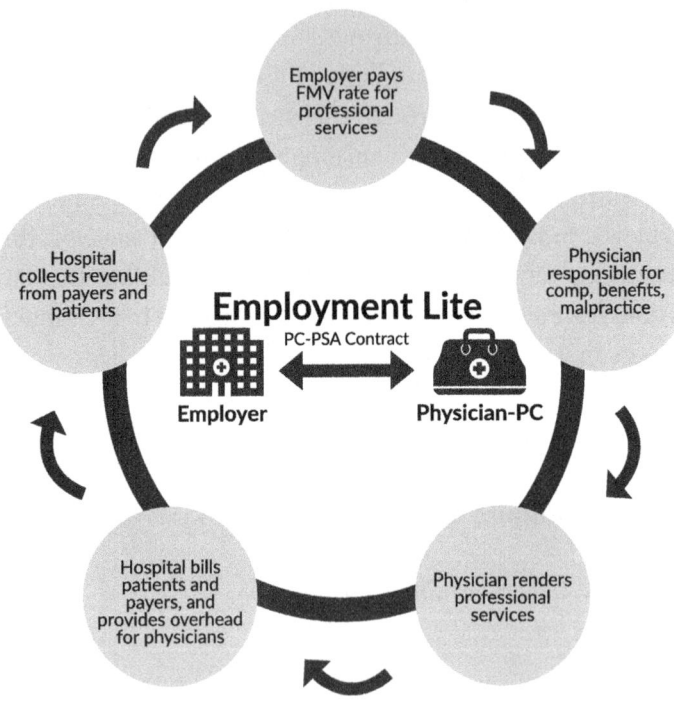

Figure 8.1

This is the most common model used to help private practice physicians transition to employment as it bridges the doctor's business interest both within and outside of an employer's safe harbor. This same bridge provides the framework for a younger generation of doctors to equally access it for their professional services that can now be deployed both inside and outside of their employer's harbor.

Generally, this is how a PC fits into this business-employment model:

Traditional Employment + PC

Locum Tenens

Locum tenens is a Latin term for "one holding the place." In this structure, your professional services are purchased or contracted out while you temporarily fill a workforce gap for a healthcare employer. The demand for these services is growing, with 85 percent of employers using them annually. Roughly 50,000 doctors, or 6 percent of the physician workforce, choose this route.[66]

This employment model is the most common independent contractor structure and has been the long-time domain of professional service agreements. If you do locums, you will have to decide on your business structure, meaning whether you want to run your locum tenens business as a sole proprietorship, partnership, LLC, or professional corporation. The best structure for you depends on your business plans.

Many locum doctors will work with a medical staffing agency that manages all the logistics, licensing, and credentialing processes associated with temporary jobs. You will typically be responsible for sourcing your own benefits, possibly malpractice insurance, and managing the small business decisions of which jobs you want to accept as well as the financial terms of the job.

---

66 Joanne Finnegan, "In Face of Physician Shortage, 85% of Healthcare Facilities Rely on Locum Tenens," Fierce Healthcare, February 27, 2020, https://www.fiercehealthcare.com/practices/face-physician-shortage-85-healthcare-facilities-rely-locum-tenens.

Doctors who do this often choose to work with a locum agency because the agency will source a host of job opportunities at predetermined financial terms that you can choose from. In turn, they will negotiate the terms of the PSA (that is technically between the agency and healthcare corporation, and you serve as the agency's subcontractor).

This model places you outside of the rigid control of a large corporate employer and insulates you from their micromanagement of your professional life. But each job will require you to conform to the unique culture and professional structure associated with your placement.

In the end, I think most doctors who go this route like the control they gain over when and where they work. They like not having to operate or manage the business side of it and, thus, outsource this piece to a locum's agency. They like not having a brick-and-mortar building, equipment, and employees. Their overhead for their professional work is self-managed and expensed out through their small business structure. The management of these expenses is, in turn, determined by your business structure and tax strategies.

From here, it's just a matter of determining how you want to receive your earned locums income in the most tax and professionally advantaged way to benefit your household. Like all independent contractors, you will receive your payment through a 1099 designation, which means you will have to pay your own taxes on the income (in comparison to W-2 income, where your employer does this for you).

I favor forming a modern version of the micro-PC for your locums' work due to its numerous tax advantages and its portability, but check with your trusted legal or accounting professional to confirm your best business structure.

I would add here that telemedicine contracting work, which is becoming more popular with physicians, would be organized in a way very similar to a locum.

Generally, this is how a PC fits into this business-employment model:

Independent Contractor +/– PC +/– Locums Agency

Direct Patient Medical Care

This model is a true medical small business model that cuts out third parties (except for hybrid models) from the equation. It proactively reinvents the historical origins of how you are compensated for your professional services, as described in Chapter 1, by cutting out middlemen and directly linking you and patients to each other. In this new frontier, big corporations no longer control you, and you are empowered to experience all the benefits of operating a small medical business that you get to define.

There is a growing enthusiasm for this among my primary care tribe, and many are joining this so-called "resistance" movement to combat the corporate takeover of medicine. Frankly, this model has a lot to like due to the way it re-empowers both you and your patient's autonomy.

However, this reimagined version of private practice places you back in the position of having to manage and operate a medical services business. This includes office space, staff, pricing and collection for your services, EHR, marketing, contracting with patients, and business plans for ancillary, lab, imaging, and pharmaceuticals. You also have to source your and your employees' benefits and cover all of your own professional overhead like malpractice insurance, licensing, equipment, and CME.

Additionally, you have to decide on your business and tax structure, such as PC, LLC, PLLC, and whether you want to be taxed as an S-Corp or C-Corp. The best design for you depends on your business plan and the advice of your legal and tax professionals. A PC with an S-Corp election is an excellent option for this architecture, just like their predecessor, the traditional private practice.

In this model, you will be self-employed as an owner-operator of your small business, such as a PC, and may receive corporate distributions or dividends depending on your tax structure. Thus your income will be a combination of salary plus distributions or dividends. The exact percentage of each is individualized, but the IRS does expect you to pay yourself what is termed a "reasonable salary" for a physician. Thus you risk an audit if you minimize your salary while maximizing your S-Corp distributions as a tax strategy. There is a sweet spot for managing this, and thus I recommend you consult with your tax professional on how to best organize it.

Depending on your business plan, PCs in this model could be shaped more like a traditional private practice PC or could be built more like the leaner modern micro-version.

Generally, this is how a PC fits into this business-employment model:

Self Employed through your corporation (PC) – any Third Parties

Private Practice

Private practices still exist in the US and can still thrive depending on the healthcare economy of its region. However, as previously stated, this model is shrinking rapidly due to the aggressive large corporate takeover of medicine and their desire to eliminate competition and control the market share of patients.

Private practices represent opportunities for large corporations to buy out and take over control of both patients and physicians for their business machinery. In essence, both are assets and fuel that produce growth in corporations, which shareholders like. Beyond large healthcare corporations, the marketplace value of private practices has led to the emergence of private equity business groups purchasing them as an asset class that they can profit from.

The corporate structure of private practices can be varied and include PCs, PLLCs (professional LLCs), LLCs, LLPs (partnerships), and PLLPs (professional partnerships).

Private practice models require you to have a business plan and financing for the startup costs, including clinical space, equipment, practice management software/EHR, etc. Additionally, you will manage staff and a host of HR services like benefit plans, oversee all of your professional components like malpractice and credentialing, marketing, and business plans associated with ancillary services and equipment. And don't forget your time-consuming and costly regulatory compliance with all aspects of your medical services, physical plant, and equipment. Wow, there is a lot involved here!

Doctors joining private practices are often provided buy-in and buy-out provisions to become shareholders of these corporations over time. The price point varies based on the size of the private practice, the economic health of the practice, and the assets owned, such as real estate.[67] For young doctors, in particular, the steep costs of the buy-in options are difficult to embrace due to their already enormous student loans. Thus, some just choose to remain employees of the small business.

Private or independent practices operate outside of the control of large corporate employers and, thus, have greater professional autonomy than their traditionally employed peers. However, you must still interface with a host of third parties, including insurances and health systems that control the players in the regional marketplace.

As those third parties saturate and control the economic playing field, they can contractually eliminate their competitors like small business private practices over time due to the shrinking revenue sources for those small practices. This is amplified by the combination of rising overhead expenses and shrinking third-party reimbursement. For instance, in the past twenty years, reimbursement for professional services is down 22 percent, and the overhead to operate a medical practice has increased by

---

[67] Jordan Frey, "5 Important Things You Need to Know about Buying into a Medical Practice," *The Prudent Plastic Surgeon* (blog), August 8, 2022, https://prudentplasticsurgeon.com/buying-into-medical-practice/.

39 percent.[68]

Corporate employers recognize these business challenges for private practices and will offer a life buoy of sorts by providing buy-out options for the individual physicians as well as their corporate private practice assets. As private practices are gradually being eliminated by large corporations, and their financial health becomes riskier, most younger doctors are opting to avoid this old-time version of physicians as traditional professional corporations.

Generally, this is how a PC fits into this business-employment model:

Employee or Self Employed through a corporation (PC) + Third Parties

As you can see, PCs are an important feature in virtually every job model that you can choose, including employment in large corporations. Therefore, it would be wise to activate this small business power that you possess at the beginning of your career so that you can maximize its value throughout Stage 2. So let's take a deeper dive into PCs to make sure you fully understand what they are and their small business value to you.

WHAT IS A PROFESSIONAL CORPORATION?

I touched on professional corporations in Chapter 1, now I am

---

68 Steven J. Cyr, "Doctors Are Not the Bad Guys," KevinMD.com, June 20, 2022, https://www.kevinmd.com/2022/06/doctors-are-not-the-bad-guys.html.

going to go a little deeper into the details of what it is and how it works. A professional corporation (PC) is an incorporated business whose shareholders are licensed to provide professional services.[69] Your independent license serves as the foundation and gives you the right to form a PC.

The owners of a professional corporation are shareholders who own stock in the business, as well as act as employees that provide professional services for the business. This is the domain of service professionals like doctors, lawyers, accountants, consultants, and architects who offer customized knowledge-based business services. Any profession that requires state licensing is eligible (or required in some states) to start a professional corporation if they wish to incorporate. However, professional corporations tend to be highly regulated at the state level, so it's important to learn your state's rules.[70]

A medical professional corporation comes with certain personal liability protection for each owner, especially when another shareholder commits malpractice. But a PC does not protect you from your own malpractice or negligence suits, thus you must still carry individual malpractice insurance (but your PC can pay for it as a business expense).

Professional corporations offer you similar advantages to a regular corporation like an LLC or PLLC including personal asset protection and tax advantages. The disadvantage includes the

---

69 "Professional Corporations," *Inc.*, accessed November 27, 2022, https://www.inc.com/encyclopedia/professional-corporations.html.

70 "State-by-State Requirements for Professional Entities in All 50 States," Northwest Registered Agent, accessed November 27, 2022, https://www.northwestregisteredagent.com/start-a-business/professional-entity-requirements.

time and money spent on corporate formalities including creating corporate bylaws, possibly managing a board of directors, having corporate officers, and holding shareholder meetings.

You must be mindful that your PC's only purpose is limited to providing professional services and, per federal guidelines, requires that substantially all (95 percent) of the business activities of the professional corporation involve services within your specific occupation. You can't run a secondary business, like a coffee shop in your lobby, for instance, without risking disqualification. However, your professional services do not have to be limited to one employer, as there are innumerable ways that a doctor's intellectual property, influence, skills, and services can be uniquely used in the marketplace.

Light bulbs may now be turning on as you survey the various medical entities in your region and how PCs may or may not fit into them. It is valuable for you to know that an individual professional corporation or partnership can also own stock and be a separate shareholder in another professional corporation as long as both belong to the same profession.

In other words, a professional corporation of doctors can't own stock in a professional corporation of lawyers, but an individual PC or group-owned PC can own shares in secondary medical ventures.

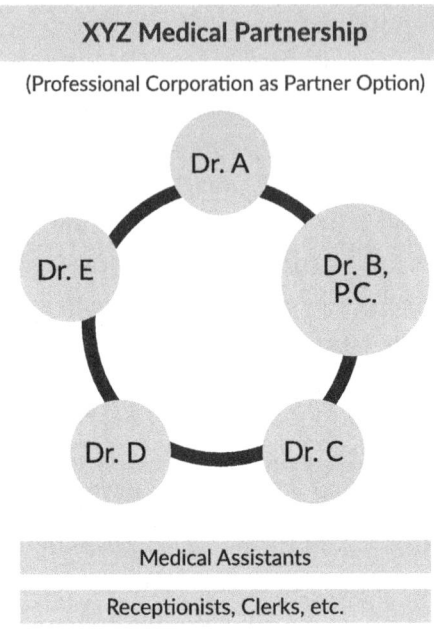

Figure 8.2

Figure 8.2 helps you visualize one iteration of the various combinations by showing how an individual PC can be a part of a partnership.

THE PARADOX

The paradox here is that I am encouraging you to form a PC while at the same time sharing the ongoing trend that PCs are becoming progressively extinct. This confounding recommendation is based on the reality that the old version of private practice PC is gradually dying, but a new type of micro-PC is emerging as the best solution to help you thrive as an employed doctor. Furthermore, this modern PC is serving as the foundation for physician marketplace adaptations that better support your well-being like direct patient care and PC-employment lite.

As I touched on in Chapter 1, when you can envision a PC outside of its old bones as a private practice, then you can begin to rethink how to maximize its power in your life. It no longer has to be a building, clinic, or physical space, rather, it can be relabeled as a professional service/small business that is driven by your specialty, derived intellectual property, and powers. Your brain and neurobiology house the massive investment associated with your long hard journey to become a doctor. Your PC ultimately serves as a business container for your earned medical intelligence, and it does not have to be constrained by a physical location.

When you reframe the structure of a PC into a virtual professional halo around an individual doctor, rather than a brick-and-mortar clinic, then you will begin to understand its potential and power for innovation.

THE ENTERPRISE MODEL

As you begin to gain confidence and experience in owning and operating your small business PC, it will often ignite entrepreneur interests in other business ventures. Your high income and built-in business power will create many opportunities and options for both passive and active income channels.

The possibilities are nearly endless for you. As you recall in

Chapter 3, options and opportunities are one of the assets that you earn by becoming a physician. With all of this in mind, most of you will develop business and income channels that ultimately land in your household to grow your net worth.

Their diversity is a strength as they tend to loosen your complete dependence on one job or one employer. The invigorating part is the sense of meaning and control that each business can provide you, which, in turn, positively affects your well-being. As you begin to assemble business assets in your portfolio, you will inevitably ask yourself, *How should I structure my multiple businesses?* This is because you likely note how there could be some economy of scale associated with these individual businesses.

I call this bigger picture the enterprise model of your business life/personal life fusion. In this larger business model, one would consider the synergy of your combined business assets and how they work together to accomplish your personal and professional goals. I am of the mindset that they should all interact in a way that ultimately helps you reach financial independence faster, but can also provide you with meaningful options for the use of your time after you retire from clinical medicine.

Along the lines of the latter, for instance, I started a non-profit regional marriage support organization called Marriage Mentors over twenty years ago and currently serve as its board president. My wife and I mentor couples through the organization, and we regularly support it financially.

Although this business venture technically costs us money (charitable contributions), it provides us meaning and purpose in Stage 2 of my career and will continue into Stage 3. It is all part of the matrix of my profit and not-for-profit business enterprise that both consumes resources and creates the assets of time and money for me.

To be honest, this book is an outcropping of this enterprise model as Dr. Inc. represents my altruistic passion project/business venture to inform and inspire physicians to understand themselves as businesses. I believe this is a critical space that needs to be forged and developed so that all physicians can thrive during Stages 2 and 3 of their career.

I have little concern about whether this passion project will make money, because its real value is that it provides meaning to me by genuinely helping my fellow physicians through the information, content, and assets that I produce for Dr. Inc. This overarching purpose for Dr. Inc. is why 50 percent of its profits are donated to charity each year.

However, I also have the wherewithal as a businessman to create an associated company called SimpliMD whose shared purpose is to help physicians thrive through the activation of their small business powers. It is a comprehensive legal, accounting, business coaching, and wealth management agency that is a turnkey option for doctors, especially with setting up PC-employment lite models.

This for-profit business venture will serve as my full-time job once I retire from clinical medicine in a few years. I expect it to make money. But because I have reached a state of financial freedom due to my enterprise model, I will feel no pressure to depend on either Dr. Inc. or SimpliMD to meet any financial obligations other than hopefully covering their overhead.

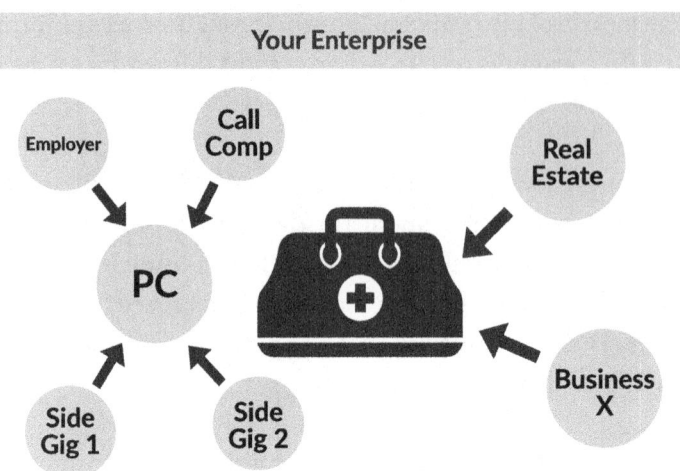

Figure 8.3

Figure 8.3 will help you visualize how your PC and your other business interests ultimately intersect in your individual household. Your own enterprise business model can be utilized to more efficiently manage all of your professional income sources, including your side jobs.

When your small business PC is combined with your passive income sources, like real estate or another business, it can be flexed to an enterprise that fully integrates each source of income.

The business, tax, and income synergy with an enterprise is fantastic as you totally control the flow of all the dollars that land in your home. Now, you are free to creatively consider all options and opportunities that will facilitate your arrival at FI and Stage 3 of your professional life.

STRUCTURING MULTIPLE BUSINESSES

As you can see, an enterprise model is a common result when you proactively organize yourself to reach financial independence and Stage 3 of your career. I don't want to go too far down this rabbit hole, but I do believe it might be helpful to mention here that there are three common ways that entrepreneurs organize their multiple businesses, and thus, you might eventually consider these as well. There are advantages and disadvantages to each approach, but I would encourage you to work with your tax, legal, or business professional to help you determine which is best for you.

1. You can create individual corporations, LLCs, or partnerships for each business. Separation reduces your liability risk but increases your operational expenses.

2. You can create fictitious names or DBAs under one corporation or LLC. This model offers the simplicity of only having one tax ID and operational expenses but has fewer legal and liability protections for the business(es).

3. You can form a holding company in which all businesses operate under one umbrella. This is often called a parent company, and it owns and operates the other businesses as subsidiaries, which remain independent legal entities. The assets and liabilities of each subsidiary business are separated from one another. This approach can be complex and expensive. It will also affect your taxes. It's best to consult an accountant or a lawyer before going this route with your multiple businesses to see if it's the right option for you.

Diversifying your income by running multiple businesses is a wonderful strategy for financial success. As a physician, your group of earned assets is the ultimate wellspring for an enterprise, and this includes your small business power of forming a PC. Your PC is a built-in high-income source that can be organized to both retain and create more income through its wise use.

As you combine the benefits of personal financial management with a disciplined personal investment plan and add in your small business power, you will begin to see the synergy of it all as your net worth grows quickly. But even more importantly, your personal and professional autonomy will grow with it.

FINANCIAL AND BUSINESS BEHAVIORS

When you proactively leverage Stages 1 and 2 of your life to reach financial independence, you will find that six common financial and business behaviors will help you get there faster. They are interrelated with the idea of the enterprise model:

1. **Be a saver.** I recommend you take 30 percent of your take-home pay and save it in various tax-advantaged and taxable accounts (based on your personal investment plan).

2. **Optimize your earning power.** Choose to activate your business powers through your PC and increase both your active income and your retained income.

3. **Invest in real estate.** First of all, learn how to maximize your cash flow in your primary residence. After that invest savings in assets that fuel your enterprise

and don't require your extra time and presence. Real estate will fuel your net worth through both the appreciation of the asset as well as the residual income it can create. If you don't want the hassle of owning real estate then consider investing in REITs (real estate investment trusts), syndications, or private equity real estate opportunities.

4. **Start a business.** The primary business for you to start is your own PC. But as your enterprise model unfolds, you will likely add others, such as an LLC for your real estate holdings.

5. **Invest in stocks.** Stocks create passive income that grows your net worth. When you take your 30 percent savings and apply it to your individual investment plan, stocks should make up 60 percent of what you are saving.

6. **Do side work.** There are multiple ways for you to earn money with side jobs using your medical degree.

Forming your own enterprise is not far-fetched because your intellectual and professional power will place you in the position to develop multiple streams of income besides your primary wages. In the next chapter, I will expound more on the active, passive, and retained income opportunities that will all eventually fuel your enterprise.

I currently have nine business entities and three professional income sources that make up my enterprise model. My PC is at the heart of my enterprise and generates the largest portion of interconnected business activity as well as the largest amount of income for my household. But it's the entire operation of the enterprise that leads to the most tax-advantaged and efficient channels of income in my household.

Using your small business superpower through a PC can take many forms in today's healthcare economy—but most importantly, it will serve as a foundation to preserve your autonomy while more rapidly growing your net worth. Both of these elements are cornerstones to thriving during Stage 2 of your career.

SUMMARY

- The modern micro-PC is built on the shoulders of its older private practice predecessor, which provides the framework for this needed market adaptation.

- You must rethink your understanding of a PC to optimize all of its modern benefits for you.

- Your individual micro-PC is the paradoxical market correction to help employed doctors thrive.

- Your PC opens the door for the development of an enterprise business model that will both increase your autonomy as well as your financial well-being.

CHAPTER 9

HOW A PC CAN HELP YOU

Enjoying autonomy at work and home tends to be a significant motive for a majority of small business owners. Having control over their lives is extremely satisfying to them. As a doctor, you share this same expectation, because autonomy is a hallmark of being called a professional. However, physicians today have discovered that their autonomy can be eroded and lost by a ruthless system that constantly seeks to control them. To avoid this, you cannot be passive about it, because the natural forces at play will always take a little bit more from you. This paradigm is especially true for employed doctors. In order to hold onto this hard-earned professional asset, it is important that each of you proactively take steps to preserve it regardless of the structure of your work environment. Starting your modern micro-PC is the most important step you can take to preserve your autonomy, due to the way this corporate structure places you back in control of your professional life.

The loss of autonomy to a system that hijacks it is noted in the "2022 Medscape Physician Burnout and Depression Report" to be among the top causes of burnout, especially for those who are traditionally employed.[71] Ultimately, while many doctors go to work each day to care for those in need, they are confronted by a system that is undermining their professional position and relegating them to the generic descriptor of "provider."

This term disparages your hard-earned professional status and corporately categorizes you like any other generic labor source that can produce income for your employer. You can combat the systemic hazards associated with losing control of your professional life by starting a PC. Of all the ways a PC can help you, preserving your professional autonomy is likely the most important one in the long run.

PRESERVING AUTONOMY

Let's briefly review, in general, how ownership of your PC will help your well-being regardless of the way you choose to use it in the marketplace. These are intangible benefits that go above and beyond the financial metrics that I will cover later in this chapter. However, since they have sufficient power to help you holistically, I propose they supersede any economic benefits that you will gain through your PC. It is up to you to decide whether your well-being, financial health, or both are most important to you.

---

71 Leslie Kane, "Physician Burnout and Depression Report 2022: Stress, Anxiety, and Anger," Medscape, January 21, 2022, https://www.medscape.com/slideshow/2022-lifestyle-burnout-6014664#4.

Let's jump into considering how starting a PC can help you by reviewing this short list of the non-economic benefits associated with owning your professional small business, most of which circulate around the idea of how it provides you more control over your life.

- **Independence.** Your individual PC is uniquely structured around you, and you have the complete power to shape and direct it. You will now own and control a professional space that your employer cannot touch. You are your own boss and have the freedom to make the decisions that are crucial to your own business success.

- **Lifestyle.** Your virtual PC is entirely portable and can go anywhere you are and thus can eliminate your "commute time" while working for your company. Traditionally, the work associated with your professional services will be in person, but the modern world of telemedicine has opened up many other doors to possibilities. Never forget that your professional brain/medical intelligence is a business power that transcends a single location. In turn, your business ownership gives you the power to determine when and where you spend your time and the freedom to truncate your work to match your family schedule.

- **Learning opportunities.** As a business owner, you will have numerous opportunities to gain an understanding of the various elements of your business plan. There is nothing like on-the-job training, and given your propensity for self-directed learning, you will love this. This is why starting your small PC while you are in training is a good idea because it fits nicely into your active learning environment and allows you to stage your business growth so that it mirrors your professional career.

- **Creative freedom.** Medicine is still an art, despite corporate medicine's best efforts to standardize quality care. There is still plenty of room for your knowledge and expertise to interface creatively with patients who are much more than biological machines. In addition to this, there is a growing list of diverse business opportunities that can use your professional skills far beyond the exam room or operating room.

- **Personal satisfaction.** It feels good to operate and run a small business predicated on your special interest in medicine. By incorporating, you are given the opportunity to pursue any of the diverse interests that you might have in connection with your profession.

As you traverse through Stage 2 of your career, you will discover that these less visible influences on your quality of life and well-being will become increasingly important. They are what will make your medical career more sustainable and provide a cadence that will help you thrive.

The built-in autonomy and control of owning your own PC will go a long way towards helping you flourish regardless of the context of how and where you use your professional services.

In addition to these intangible benefits of personal and professional autonomy that a modern PC can bring to your life, it will also provide you with tangible benefits that especially enhance your financial health.

ENHANCING YOUR FINANCIAL HEALTH

In comparison to receiving your income as a traditional W-2 employee, receiving the same income through your modern PC will grow your annual household net worth by 10-15 percent or more. That is because it places you in control of the flow of dollars from your earnings, and thus, you can diversify and expand your professional and personal options as to how those dollars benefit your household.

An option can be defined as something that can be chosen, such as an alternative course of action, or an addition to or replacement of a standard course. Small businesses and their owners—by definition—are imbued with the power to control the flow of their dollars in ways that are not available to the traditional employee.

While the financial benefits of owning your PC will improve your financial health regardless of the job structure with which you use it, I am going to discuss this topic from the vantage point of PC-employment lite in particular.

As you recall from Chapter 3, one of the assets that you earned in your professional journey was *options and opportunities*. When you form your own PC and begin using it, you now have a place for this valuable asset to be housed and activated.

If you convert from traditional employment to PC-employment lite, there will be numerous options and opportunities that will be restored to you through the business power of your PC.

Regardless of whether you are preserving or restoring your options and opportunities through a PC, there are four broad economic areas through which your small business can enhance your financial health:

1. Income diversification

2. Tax strategies

3. Individualized fringe benefits

4. Retirement funding

There is a whole lot here to consider, so I am going to take a bit of time to unpack each of these elements. Let's begin with your income since it tends to be the most significant influencer of your net worth and financial well-being.

Your most common and consistent income source is the compensation that you earn at your primary job. This active source of income has to mirror the enlarging and dynamic expenses associated with your growing household and lifestyle needs during Stage 2 of your career. Due to these latter forces, you will often have to consider options to bring more money into your home.

Growing Your Income within Employment

For the traditional employee, the subject of compensation commonly comes up with your first or second contract extension, the timing of which often correlates with your enlarging household spending that is associated with the early part of Stage 2 of your career. Children alone amp this up with the current cost per child to a middle-income married couple being an extra $14,800 per year and an eighteen-year total of $267,000.[72]

Whether it is due to children, cars, a home, vacations, or loans, you will likely find yourself looking for ways to grow the flow of dollars into your home.

Your first response will typically be to figure out how you can increase your income through your job. Your employer will typically first point you towards the opportunity connected to productivity-based compensation models that incentivize you to earn more income by producing more wRVUs. It's a pretty simple formula: do more work for your employer and they will pay you more money.

They will note that they are constrained by federal laws to keep your compensation within a fair market range, and thus can't negotiate an increase in your productivity-based compensation. This is the fundamental reason they have a productivity-based compensation matrix. Additionally, it would be unfair to your fellow employed doctors if they used compensation formulas that are different for each doctor. This type of variance would also place both of you at risk of penalties for breaking federal laws regarding physician compensation.

Therefore, the first level of conversations will circulate around steps you can take to make you more productive and efficient including the standard mantra of "just adding one more patient per day."

---

72 "How Much Does It Cost to Raise a Child?," Western & Southern Financial Group, last modified October 19, 2021, https://www.westernsouthern.com/learn/financial-education/how-much-does-it-cost-to-raise-a-kid.

You can increase your income through this process, but ultimately your workload in your primary job does have a productivity ceiling, so wedging more work through your work week has its limitations.

In anticipation of this conundrum, your employer will often create a menu of extra income options that will allow them to pay you more in exchange for additional services that you can perform for their corporation. These can include things like productivity bonuses, quality bonuses, medical directorships, mid-level supervision, hospital call, medical education, research, and leadership-governance roles. Each of these additional opportunities will increase your earned income through your employer, and will typically be ADDED to your current patient care workload.

The route of growing income by working within the employer's harbor is what most will do to address the needs of their home. It's convenient and simply channels the additional income through their current paycheck. For traditional employees, due to their heavy alignment with a single employer, that employer often is their sole source for creating more income. If that employer is unable to meet the income needs, choosing a new employer who can become a viable option.

However, let me warn you regardless of who you work for, if your pay flows through to you as a W-2 individual tax entity, based on the tiered tax codes, your extra income may not actually net you as much household gain as you think. I will go into greater detail with this later when I discuss taxes.

In contrast to the singular employer source that traditional employees must use to increase their household dollars, micro-PC owners have more diverse and sophisticated options for meeting their growing household needs.

Much like their traditional peers, they can earn more money through extra work through their primary employer. This extra income ends up being even more beneficial when it flows through a PC-employment lite structure because the household will get to hold onto more of these earned dollars.

But beyond making more money via a single income source like traditional employees, a PC can more aptly increase the diversity of income sources that will help meet your household needs. This diversity is a strength for small businesses and, ultimately, reduces your interdependence on a single source of income. Within this PC business model, your household dollars can grow efficiently through all three income sources: retained, active, and passive income.

As you consider these sources and how they increase your financial position, I would encourage you to reflect on which opportunity(s) will require more of your time or physical presence. In the end, choosing sources that conserve your time is probably your most important consideration. I like how Warren Buffet states this idea when he says, "The rich invest in time, and the poor invest in money."

INCOME DIVERSIFICATION

Retained Income

Retained earnings for the medical professional are rarely spoken about, mainly because they are assumed to not apply to individuals;

rather, they are thought to primarily apply to businesses. But as you recall, you have a special power to be considered an individual business, and thus, this door is opened up for you.

If you Google search this term right now, you won't find a whole lot of hits on individuals retaining income, but you will find a mountain of content on how companies can hold onto more of their profits. For companies, this is an accounting term that describes the methods associated with keeping more of the company's earnings.

A business's net earnings are the bottom box in the accounting ledger after its fiduciary obligations are met, including distributing dividends to shareholders. The multiple filtering channels of corporate revenue can be likened to the filtering that occurs with our large paychecks. The flow of your cash through this system of filters creates opportunities to retain some of that income.

In traditional employment as a W-2 wage earner, you have very little opportunity to alter the filters, but you do have an opportunity annually to retain these dollars when you file your taxes via the system of itemized deductions that lead to a "tax refund check."

Yet, frustratingly, the number of opportunities for high-income W-2 tax-advantaged income retention is gradually being reduced through our tax code as it disproportionately taxes those who earn a high income.

While there are some tax-advantaged benefits and professional overhead deductions available to W-2 employees, many items must be paid for out of your after-tax dollars. A classic example of this would be unreimbursed CME expenses.

The most valuable element of this relatively unknown income category to most doctors is that it doesn't take any more of your time or energy to access it. You don't have to work more, longer, or harder to add these dollars to your household. It's kind of like free money, but you just have to have the business system in place to help you retain it.

Most doctors can keep up to 15 percent of their gross income by doing this. I retained $70,000 when I activated these small business channels, as detailed in Chapter 6. SimpliMD offers a quick and free retained income questionnaire at their website if you want to check out an estimate on how much money a PC-employment lite model can help you to hold onto at your current income level.[73]

Active Income

For physicians, active income is mainly built around your professional services, professional state, or your intellectual property (medical brain). It's not that you can't have non-professional forms of active income, but the $/hour rate will rarely be equivalent to the value of your professional services. Thus, I suggest you stay in your professional lane to maximize this income.

Active income involves work that requires your time and presence for the money to be earned. This does include your primary job, and it also includes extra income sources that your employer can create for you or opportunities that you can source for yourself.

---

73 "Retained Income Questionnaire," SimpliMD, accessed November 27, 2022, https://simplimd.com/questionnaire/.

All sources of your active professional income can flow in through your PC, even if your primary job doesn't. In fact, I would suggest that using a micro-PC for your side jobs would be the most common initial setup configuration for the majority of employed doctors, including residents.

Let's look at a specific example of what this would look like if you used your PC only for your side income.

Suppose you are a married, traditionally employed W-2 physician making $300,000 per year and you were adding $40,000 of side income to your household. As W-2 income, the $40K would be taxed at a higher rate because it's simply added to your total wages; at a marginal tax rate of 24 percent, your household would only receive $30,000 of this extra income.

However, if you form a micro-PC and funnel this income through your PC, you will save nearly $10,000 in taxes compared to receiving it as W-2 income. You will also financially benefit your household more effectively than if you simply added it to your paycheck.

For example, you could end up with a solo 401(k) of nearly $25,000, a profit-sharing distribution of $5,000, and potentially add $8,500 of untaxed income to your household via a dwelling unit program. In other words, your household would hold onto $38,500 of this $40,000 side income, which is a whopping difference of $8,500 more than if you added the same money to your W-2 salary. These numbers demonstrate the impressive financial benefits of opening up a PC to run your professional side income through, even if you are traditionally employed.

There is a long list of side jobs that you can pursue through your micro-PC, outside of your primary employer, to earn extra income for your household. However, be sure to keep your time constraint considerations in mind. Over-committing to side work can create unneeded stress and fatigue. Fundamentally, all active income sources are professional opportunities that require your time and presence. So carefully evaluate what you can safely add to your plate in regard to your well-being. Active professional income can include a host of non-clinical, clinical, education or influencing, and coaching opportunities, just to name a few.

It is valuable to form a micro-PC if you are an attending physician and 5-10 percent of your household dollars are derived annually from side income. In other words, if you currently do or have the potential for side income at these levels or higher, then setting up a micro-PC is financially viable for you. However, flowing all of your active professional income through your PC is the most ideal way to maximize your earned dollars. That is why I highly recommend the PC-employment lite model.

Passive Income

Passive income includes regular earnings from a source other than an employer or contractor. Technically, the Internal Revenue Service (IRS) says passive income can come from two sources: rental property or a business in which one does not actively participate, such as being paid book royalties or stock dividends.

Traditionally, employed doctors can use their high income to create passive income channels; therefore, you don't have to own a PC to do this. The most common tax-advantaged passive income channels that you will build into your portfolio are stock market-based retirement funds such as your 401(k), 403(b), 457, and IRAs through your employer. You may also have other taxable brokerage accounts that are part of your savings plan. Unlike starting a business or buying real estate, these passive income sources won't require more of your time.

However, when you flow all of your professional service income through your PC and thus take over managing your own benefit plan, you will have a deeper tax-advantaged wellspring of funds to use to build your passive income portfolio. The extra household income generated through your PC's retained earnings can and should be translated into passive income sources for you. This is how passive income is linked beneficially to your PC, due to its net effect of increasing your investible household dollars.

Passive income is an important source of income that should be assembled in your portfolio because of the way it grows your net worth. In their purest form, this represents how you can earn money without requiring your time or physical presence—passive income works for you even when you're not working.

Real estate is one of the most common sources of passive income for doctors, and it has been a personal favorite of mine. It fits nicely into the enterprise model and provides an excellent combination of asset growth and simultaneous income when appropriately managed.

It is especially powerful when it can be tied into your professional practice via a medical office building. However, starting a business and certain types of real estate will require your time and presence. Thus, although they are considered passive due to the way that money flows into your household, they are hardly passive in terms of your time and energy. The appeal of passive income is that it is more scalable than your professional services and thus has fewer limits. In other words, your active professional income has a ceiling that is created by your singular ability to do the work. But because passive income does not require your time and presence, you no longer are the limiting factor on the size and scope of those passive income sources.

It is noteworthy that passive income sources are typically separate business entities outside of the scope of your PC and professional services. Thus they will be legally separate from your PC and function within the broader enterprise model reviewed in Chapter 8.

TAXES

Choosing which entity will receive your income is the most important decision you will make in regard to your tax strategies. Receiving your professional compensation as 1099 income through a PC multiplies your options for income retention, while receiving it as a W-2 individual significantly reduces your options to the point that it is relegated to a shrinking menu of tax-advantaged individual programs.

Taxes make up the largest pool from which you can draw upon to place money back into your household. I am not talking about avoiding taxes, rather, I am talking about how you can wisely regain some of what will be taken from you.

For example, our government rewards certain social behavior within the tax code by providing tax credits (deductions) that allow you to gain back some of your money. Simple examples of this are having children, marriage, home ownership, and charitable donations.

So let's dive in and briefly review this area in the context of comparing individual W-2 wage earners and the owner-operators of PCs.

Individual and Business Tax Advantages

Through the PC structure, you can lower both your effective and marginal tax rates by lowering your individual W-2 wages. Your employer will pay your PC the 1099 income you earn via your professional services agreement, and then your PC will pay you for those services performed on behalf of your own company.

Your salary as an owner-employee of the PC must meet the IRS definition of a reasonable market rate. Small business people are known to exploit the tax arbitrage of individual versus corporate earnings and, in the process, keep their individual tax rate low. They lower their salary to a very low rate and then receive household income through their corporate shareholder distributions. This mix is a common strategy to reduce their overall effective tax rate.

I don't recommend you dramatically lower the value of your earnings because the IRS knows of your expected high income as a doctor. An artificially low salary from your PC will not comply with the IRS definition of "reasonable market salary" and could result in an audit and penalty for tax fraud. There is no need to dramatically lower your W-2 salary within this business model, so make sure to consult with a professional to ensure it is safely on the lower side of reasonable.

However, as discussed earlier, there is a fair market income range for your professional services, and within your own company, I suggest you pay yourself the LOWER range of that market rate. Not to confuse things here, but you will also be negotiating with your large corporate employer for them to pay your PC at the HIGHEST fair market value rate for your professional services. Your business (and thus, you) will benefit from the difference between the two rates.

Another example of how a PC can benefit your household's financial state via the interplay of your individual taxes and your business operations is the IRS's Augusta Rule. This tax-free rental exemption allows homeowners to rent their home for up to fourteen days per year without needing to report that rental income on their individual tax returns.

This rule applies to any taxpayer who owns a home in the United States as long as your home is not your primary place of business. Your PC can rent your own home from you for business meetings at a market rate. The rent amounts to tax-free income for your household that is flowed through your business. I would add that this small business advantage should be carefully deployed under the guidance of your legal and accounting professionals to make sure that it is done properly.

Individual Taxes

Whether you are traditionally employed or own your own PC, you will be compensated for your professional services via individual W-2 earnings. The payroll source for traditional employees is your large employer, and for your self-employment through your PC, it is your small business corporation. The same federal, state, and local tax obligations will be equally applied to both checks, and it is the responsibility of the corporation to make this happen and pay the specific parties this money. For small businesses, these taxes are paid via a system of estimated quarterly taxes that you will be responsible for calculating or working with your accountant to calculate.

As an individual within the US tax code, you have a small menu of tax-advantaged options or strategies for retaining any of your W-2 income from your tax obligations. This includes a host of itemized deductions that have previously been mentioned, but there are other common solutions for you and your spouse to consider. They include:

1. Start your own business

2. Tax loss harvesting of investments

3. If you own real estate, you can declare real estate professional status, which allows for writing off passive real estate loss, among other things. This is commonly the role of the doctor's spouse but also has rigid IRS guidelines associated with it.

4. Maximized tax-advantaged retirement accounts and investments

The term "tax-advantaged" refers to any type of investment, financial account, or savings plan that is either exempt from taxation, tax-deferred, or offers other types of tax benefits. Examples of tax-deferred investments are IRAs and 401(k) 403(b) and 457 plans. Examples of tax-free accounts are Roth IRAs, Roth 401(k) s, and 529 education plans. Tax-advantaged investments include municipal bonds and real estate depreciation.

The real challenge is that Uncle Sam has placed caps on each of these, and once you have maxed out the federal limits on these tax-advantaged options, you have only a few other options remaining to tap into. These include having a child, daycare credit, mortgage interest, home office deduction, and charitable giving to name a few of the more common ones.

Corporate Taxes

When you start your own PC, your earnings will come in via 1099 income that can now flow into a series of filters that include you as an individual. The tax strategies mentioned above still apply to your individual W-2 earnings derived from your PC-based salary.

Your small business PC opens up more opportunities for tax strategies in addition to you as an individual.

PC and Employment Lite

You Have Options in the Tax Code

	Employee Taxation	Pass-Through Taxation	Large Co. Taxation
	Individual	S-Corp	C-Corp
Tax Rate Control	None	Medium	High
Pre-Tax Savings	Low	Medium	High
Pre-Tax Benefits	Low	Medium	High

Figure 9.1

As you can see in Figure 9.1, your earnings now have multiple tax channels available to them within your PC small business structure that are not available to the individual taxpayer. Generally speaking, corporate taxes are lower than the tax rates associated with high-income earners. Due to the complexity of the ever-changing tax code for both individuals and corporations, it is beyond the scope of this book to be more specific about those tax rates. I suggest you work closely with an accounting, legal, or business professional to optimize the tax-advantaged flow of your earnings.

INDIVIDUALIZED FRINGE BENEFITS

The fact is that as a traditional employee, you pay a growing portion of your employer's benefit plan and yet have little or no control over how it is organized to meet your needs. The result is that you pay for things you don't need, you will come up short on your tax-advantaged retirement funds, and you will miss out on fringe benefits that you could use for your family. Although your employer's benefit plan is turnkey for traditional employees and usually comprehensive, it has significant limitations because it cannot be individualized for you and your family. Those limitations may not seem all that significant on the surface, but as we will unpack, it does have important implications for you.

When you transition to a PC-employment lite contract, you gain full control over the sourcing and creation of a benefit plan that is designed to individually benefit you and your household. In contrast to large employers, small businesses are able to provide their owners a host of unique benefits that include automobile expenses, unrestricted continuing medical education, cell phone-digital services, business expenses, home office expenses, private school reimbursement, employment of family members, health, life, and disability insurance, as well as unique retirement plans that allow for larger contributions than traditional employment contracts. Each benefit can be crafted around the needs of you and your family. Therefore your business only pays for the benefits you need.

Ultimately, the fringe benefit plan offered to you from your PC should be designed specifically to benefit you and your household, and in turn, they are underwritten by the tax-advantaged framework of your individual PC business structure.

RETIREMENT FUNDING

The three-legged stool has been a commonly used image associated with retirement planning. The three legs represent three general sources of retirement income, which include a pension, social security, and your savings (investments). In recent years, corporate pensions have largely been replaced by 401(k) plans and the like, which can be either employee funded, employer-funded, or both.

I won't digress into the solvency of the social security fund for providing money for your retirement, but it is fair to say that it may be best to plan as though you can't depend on it. This will leave you with employer-based retirement plans in combination with your savings (investments) to fund your retirement.

When you are a traditional employee, you will be limited to the amount you can save in tax-advantaged contributions to your retirement accounts. Because of ERISA, in 2023, this is currently $66,000 if you are under fifty (a combination of employer and individual contribution).

Using some simple math, if you maxed this out with every paycheck, the thirty-year total (without growth or interest) of the basis would be $1,980,000. Although that is a lot of money, it will fall short of the estimated needed nest egg for most physicians, which is roughly $3–5 million.

When I was a traditional employee, I used to naively believe that maxing out my retirement contributions would be enough. Unfortunately, I think many of you assume the same thing as you trust in the wisdom of our federal government and your employer to organize this for you. This is especially common early in your career and is easily missed if you don't monitor your net worth regularly.

One of the greatest benefits to opening your PC is that both you and your spouse (if your PC employs him/her) now have the opportunity to set up an individual defined benefit plan (like a cash balance plan) that allows for tax-advantaged contributions well over $200,000 annually (amount is based upon actuarial tables and will be proportional to the size of your 1099 income flowing into your PC). This is over three times the basis amount compared to a traditional employee and easily meets the estimated funds that you will need for retirement.

PCS GROW YOUR HOUSEHOLD DOLLARS AND NET WORTH

In the end, deploying and maximizing all of the Stage 1 assets you have earned and enveloping them in your own micro-PC with an employment lite agreement will result in many advantages, including enhanced autonomy and accelerated growth of your net worth during Stage 2. In turn, this will allow you to arrive at Stage 3 earlier than you would via traditional employment.

Let me share a real-world example of what all of this looks like. Chris and I practice in similar specialties within the same state. He reached out to me and asked if we could have dinner with our spouses and talk about my professional business structure. He had heard about it from a friend.

Chris had been working as an employed doctor for his hospital for nearly twenty years but was interested in how my business discoveries might help him retain more of his income.

After completing a feasibility evaluation through SimpliMD that affirmed that he would see significant retained income, he formed his PC and converted it to an employment lite contract. With innovative business structuring under SimpliMD's guidance, he was able to retain more than $150,000 in tax-advantaged income annually. His savings were compounded by his ability to receive benefits through his wife's job, saving him an additional $20,000 each year. Using an enterprise model, he was able to incorporate his vacation home and woodworking hobby, as well as his wife's knitting business, into the total business structure.

Additionally, evaluation of his hospital employer's compensation plan led to a sizable raise as it was not at a fair market rate. The end result was Chris being paid more for his professional services through his PC.

By changing how Chris's income flowed into his home through his PC rather than as an individual taxpayer and maximizing his supporting business structure, it became a home run for him. He now has a much more robust business structure that will provide him with many more options for maximizing his earnings while benefiting his household and quickly growing his net worth.

Chris is not a select case, and a similar experience is also available to you. Doctors give up a lot of money, autonomy, and time by blindly trusting their employer and not proactively leveraging their earned assets into their personal and professional life. Your biggest mistake is not to start your PC, even though you have earned the right and privilege to do it.

The concept of an employed doctor owning their own medical business is counterintuitive to most and, thus, remains hidden from view. Now that I have revealed this option to you, your next step is to do what Chris and I have done with a PC-employment lite job structure.

Unfortunately, this is not a unilateral decision on your part, as your large corporate employer will also need to cooperate with you on this novel job structure. You should be warned that you are likely to meet resistance to this proposed change to their preferred status quo of traditional employment. In the next chapter, we'll discuss these so-called gatekeepers further, and review how you can overcome their impedance.

SUMMARY

- A micro-PC will help diversify the income sources into your household.

- Your micro-PC provides you with many options to add income to your household.

- Retained income is the best way to add dollars to your home because it requires no extra time or work from you.

- Micro-PCs allow for tax strategies not available to the individual.

- Your micro-PC will allow you to reach Stage 3 of your career faster.

CHAPTER 10

THE GATEKEEPERS

A GATEKEEPER IS SOMEONE WHO HAS THE POWER TO DECIDE who receives access to particular resources and opportunities and who does not. Gatekeepers are people or policies who act as a go-between, controlling access from one point to another while preventing unwanted entry or intrusion.

There are multiple stakeholders and gatekeepers in your professional workplace playing field, and I believe it will be valuable for you to understand who they are and what powers they wield to potentially block you.

Ultimately, there are multiple sources of resistance connected to the systemic changes that PC-employment lite causes within the realm of physician employment. I know from coaching scores of physicians that doctors are often eager to embrace this idea, only to have it shut down by a gatekeeper somewhere along the line.

My experience is that the larger the corporate employer, the stiffer and more multi-layered the gatekeeping is.

As a result, change, individuation, and innovation are often quickly blocked by large employers who prefer not to change an employment structure that favors them in its current state. Instead, they would prefer to spend millions of dollars on physician well-being programs that only offer doctors solutions to address their resiliency skills rather than looking at systemic solutions that will allow their employed doctors to thrive. In many regards, they would prefer us to learn how to mindfully adapt to the pain of a broken system rather than fix what is broken.

Even with their multi-layered resistance, no administrator can stop you from forming your PC and using it outside of the contractual terms of your employment harbor.

You should expect that most gatekeepers will not embrace the idea of you using your PC within your employment model. To them, it will feel like you are asking them to allow for small business competition within their safe harbor.

But before we get to employers, you must take a hard look at yourself in the mirror because you are the first gatekeeper you will encounter.

As a licensed medical professional, no one other than yourself can keep you from forming a PC. You have the absolute power and authority to do this, no matter your current employment status. You simply have to decide if it is an asset you want to turn on now, later, or never.

RESISTANCE FROM SELF AND PEERS

You are conditioned to trust and follow your cohorts during your training and practice years. They serve as a rich repository of coaching on how to learn, behave, and live like a doctor. The built-in hierarchy of your medical training process engenders this behavior. In that arena, you quickly figure out how to think like your superiors and peers to maximize your learning, reduce conflicts, and get a better grade. Outliers don't prosper in the medical training crucible, but conformers keep on moving up the chain.

Some would call this learning by following, others would call it survival by conforming. There is typically safety in numbers, and if you tuck in closely with your peers, you will be carried along with them to your destination. Truthfully, medical professionals are often shaped by this herd mentality that reinforces uniformity of thinking and behaving.

For those who are beginning to wrap up their residency training, they will continue to look to their residency peers for advice and counsel as they search for a job and start their attending physician career. Comparing and contrasting recruitment experiences and job searches creates a bond with your cohort.

This herd-like conditioning influences why such an overwhelming majority of new graduates choose employment: quite simply, it's because their peers are doing it.

However, once you choose your preferred job, you will separate from your trusted peers and begin operating as an individual business person in the marketplace. Here your employer will have the upper hand as they isolate you and set the ground rules and structure of the business relationship they will have with you.

Since your medical school and residency didn't equip you with the business skills needed at this phase, you will be left to manage this independently. In addition, due to the confidential nature of contracts and salaries among attending physicians, you will likely no longer lean on your peers to compare things.

RESISTANCE TO RETHINK

I get it, you have been trained to see yourself as a doctor and not as a business person. You have been conditioned to blindly accept the goodwill of your employer with whom you entrusted your specialty training. It would be easy to assume that all employers are actively interested in your professional development.

Until you embrace the fact that you are a business, and therefore, you are a business person, you will blindly follow the path of your peers. In this space, the idea of hiring a professional agent to represent you, forming a PC, and using a PC-employment lite contract is not typically considered due to their business-like overtones. It's just not in your wheelhouse.

Thus, these new ideas about your professional future involving operating a PC will be rather disruptive to your herd mentality, and you have been conditioned not to be an outlier.

Rather than teaching you a new medical skill, I am trying to expose you to a new way of thinking about yourself professionally. This rethinking of your professional assets, PCs, and employment models are too novel to be mainstream at this point. Thus you will have to evaluate it through the keyhole of what's best for you, and this separation from your peers may prove too psychologically difficult for you.

Ultimately, it is always easier to follow the path of least resistance. In your case, that means choosing to sideline a number of your earned professional assets and exchanging them for a traditional employment contract. This is the default, and as you follow the well-worn path of your friends, it is where you will land. It's up to you to decide if you are willing to re-think your professional life and reorganize your earned assets into a more progressive employment structure.

All or Nothing

If you are already in a traditional employment contract, this will be one of the most common reasons that you, as a new attending, will choose not to start your PC. You believe since it doesn't apply to your current contract that a PC won't help you right now. Don't fall into the trap of thinking that this has to be an all-or-nothing commitment to this business model of PC-employment lite.

A better way to look at it is as a staged commitment that will be progressively worked out in your professional life. Take employment, for example. If you have a traditional employment contract and this is unlikely to change soon, it does not mean a micro-PC will not benefit you. Although forming a PC is fundamental to having an employment lite agreement, the opposite is not true.

In other words, the lack of a PC-employment lite agreement does not preclude the benefits of starting your micro-PC. Don't let your employer dictate whether forming a PC is right for you, as any resistance you receive from them doesn't have to block your small business resolve. As outlined earlier, the benefits and opportunities associated with deploying this earned asset are so high that its formation is not exclusively dependent upon having a PC-employment lite agreement.

Fear of Running a Business

Your biggest mistake as a young doctor is to read about starting your PC, affirm its value, and then fail to act on it due to your perception that you are unable to run a business. You aren't equipped with a business education, and thus, you fear failing at your PC due to the complexities and challenges of operating a small business. This fear can be easily overcome by outsourcing the management to a physician-centric agency that can help you create, maintain, and use your PC. Since you are by nature a quick learner and due to your coachability, you are likely to catch onto the skills quickly.

From my experience with coaching doctors, I can tell you that it doesn't take long for them to understand the case of operating their PC. They also rapidly begin experiencing the power of their small business to help restore their autonomy and to improve their household income.

In the end, although there are reasons that doctors will be resistant to forming a PC, after evaluating the risks and benefits of using this earned asset for themselves, they are often interested and want to move forward. This is especially true with a PC-employment lite model.

But, as you embrace your PC superpower and try to move forward with it, there will be others who resist this process as gatekeepers. You will need to be prepared for why they may resist your entry into the business of medicine.

RESISTANCE FROM BUSINESS MANAGERS

Dr. Raj is a practicing private practice dermatologist who just built a beautiful new medical office building to house his growing dermatology practice that was organized as a PC from the beginning. He fully understood the economic value of a PC, but he was concerned that his enterprise was not maximizing its tax strategies from a business standpoint, so he reached out to me.

After carefully evaluating his assets, we both determined that he would retain a significant amount of his earned income if he wrapped his business assets into a more efficient business model. It was clear he would benefit from changing how his assets interacted together as a whole. However, when his business manager got involved, he shut down the entire process, suggesting he was concerned about the safety and credibility of the business structuring, even though the business model has a proven track record.

Ultimately, he was threatened by the innovative recommendations that exposed his limited skill set as a business manager and therefore he pushed Dr. Raj away from it. Being forced to choose between going with the advice of his business manager friend, or a national physician agency, he leaned towards his friend. This is understandable, but it is a missed opportunity for him. He'll be ok in his current business model that was structured around a PC and his medical office building, but the lost retained income may haunt him later.

Beyond the single-member PC and their business manager, medical directors of partnerships and larger private practices fear how this novel packaging of an individual physician within a micro-PC envelope could disrupt their corporations. The following is a real-world example of that scenario.

Andy is a very successful spine surgeon who had recently switched jobs and joined a large orthopedic group. He was in his first few years of the partnership, and there were older managing partners in the group who controlled the business operations. I met with him after he reached out to get more information about how he could increase his retained income. After the SimpliMD agency completed a feasibility study, it revealed that he could see as much as $200,000 in retained income annually through a PC-based business wrap-around, and this made him eager to implement it.

The simple movement from him individually owning the partnership shares meant his income would now be shifted to his personal small business PC. It would be a simple change allowing his income to flow through to his PC first, rather than him personally. Visually it looked like this in Figure 10.1.

However, Andy's managing partners shut it down, fearing the change could lead to unfair advantages, disunity, and an unequal partnership between doctors who were organized in this novel way and those who weren't. Unfortunately, their unfounded fear about this innovative business model proved to be an obstacle to something that could potentially help all the group members.

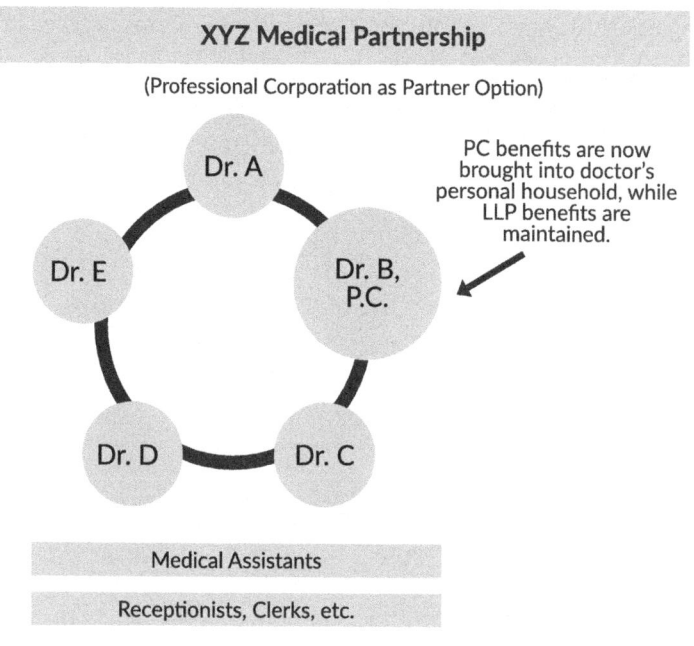

Figure 10.1

The point is that gatekeepers are not just found within the realm of employed doctors but can also be encountered in virtually any practice environment, including private practice. Even in this space, the fear of disrupting the status quo is a common obstacle.

Beyond individual practices and partnerships, the most common scenario is when a large corporate employer is resistant to the idea of using a PC-employment lite contract rather than a traditional one.

RESISTANCE FROM LARGE EMPLOYERS

Most large employers are interested in mitigating their risks as they operate a safe harbor for their physician employees. They take compliance with all the legal obligations associated with your employment and professional services very seriously. In the long run, this should create a great sense of security for you as you don't have to fear breaking any federal or state laws associated with your practice of medicine.

Enforcement of these laws has objective and subjective components, so most employers (wisely) are careful to steer clear of the gray spaces associated with them.

Ultimately, this creates an "in the box" thinking for most employers that translates into standardized contracts and rigid employment policies.

This is the backdrop for their response when you ask to do something outside their normal employment box, like a PC-employment lite contract. If the idea is new to them, they will likely resist providing it to you.

This is where having a credible agent or lawyer representing you can prove extremely helpful. Hearing about the legitimacy of something new or innovative like this will be accepted much more readily by a credible source than if you are representing yourself and saying, "I read about it in a book or on a blog." Although one of my end goals of this book is to make it a credible resource for both doctors and employers to understand and use in the employment journey, it may be a little much to ask your employer to read this book as part of your negotiation, but that is an option!

Suppose your employer pushes back on this idea and is not receptive to interjecting the simple change of adding a PC to your name in the employment contract. In that case, I recommend you at least ask to add an option provision within your contract to revisit this discussion at your next contract renewal.

Although you might meet some resistance to the idea of a PC and employment lite with your employer, I believe the most strategic way to winsomely communicate about this is to frame it as a systemic solution to the physician burnout crisis. In reality, most employers are looking for burnout solutions, and this newer employment model's simplicity will prove to be the least disruptive and least costly option.

I was speaking to a medical director of a physician network this past year and proposed that a PC-employment lite conversion for their more productive physicians could serve as both a physician retention initiative as well as an intervention to reduce physician burnout. I suggested she consider a pilot study of five physicians on this model.

They could track various elements of the pilot program ranging from cost savings to the employer, productivity, economic benefits to the doctor, physician satisfaction, retention, and physician well-being scores. The director was very interested in this innovative idea; however, when she took it to her superiors further up in the organization, she was told it could not be done because they wanted all employed doctors in the network to have the same standardized contract. This is an excellent example of the resistance to change within organizations, especially larger inflexible ones.

Although employers have no control over your formation of a PC, ultimately, they fear that your PC signals your intent to compete with them within the marketplace in your medical service line. Although this is not the case, clearing this up through contractual terms can sometimes help curb this fear. This will often quell their concerns about the risks of letting you activate your PC while you reside in their safe harbor.

In regard to PC-employment lite, employers primarily fear losing control of you. The tight alignment of your professional life and small business superpower is fundamental to their interest in you. Your formation of a PC and an employment lite agreement communicates to them that you have become more aware of your small business powers. Thus, they fear its development in your professional life. Ultimately, your small business growth could lead to you leaving their employment. Since it is estimated to cost employers between $250,000 and $1 million to replace a doctor, this is a significant concern for them.[74]

As you discuss it with an employer, make sure to keep the conversation centered on your professional services. This is why they are interested in you, and whether they receive them as an individual or via your PC should make no difference. Your business model of delivering those services is your prerogative, not theirs.

WIN-WIN

One of the most noteworthy features of this innovative idea of PC-employment lite is that it allows for there to truly be a win-win business relationship created out of it.

---

74 "The Cost of Turnover in Dollars," *Medical Economics*, September 13, 2016, https://www.medicaleconomics.com/view/the-cost-of-turnover-in-dollars.

Figure 10.2 summarizes many of the benefits that both employers and physicians receive from employment lite.

Employment Lite

Benefits to Physician	Benefits to Employer
Greater professional autonomy and control	Greater physician recruitment and retention through the program
Greater retained household earnings	Increase physician household income without paying them more
Better individualized fringe benefits program	Organizational cost savings due to paying less employment expenses including benefits
Increased retirement savings through SimpliMD program	Emancipate physicians from ERISA restrictions on employee retirement funding
Simple transition process for doctors through agency outsourcing to SimpliMD	Opportunity for employers to reduce overhead and expenses associated with physician employment through innovative model offered by SimpliMD
No job change with invisible transition with same employer	Maintain market share of patients via highly aligned physician employment model. Seamless transition other than paycheck now issued to the doctor's PC (1099), rather the individual doctor (W-2)
Burnout prevention via enhanced physician control over their professional and personal life	Reduce physician burnout through a novel model that restores physician control over their lives while saving the employer money

Figure 10.2

With this transition, employers will end up with more happy, more productive doctors who are more likely to be retained by the organization and more likely to help attract more recruited doctors to join them due to professional and personal satisfaction.

Additionally, in an age where employers struggle to keep up with growing physician salaries, this arrangement REDUCES their employment expenses while simultaneously supporting your ability to retain more of your hard-earned income. The end effect is that your employer is giving you a raise while their business expenses for your services are cut (they shed paying for your benefit plan and payroll taxes). This jaw-dropping combination almost seems too good to be true. It's truly a mic-drop moment for both parties.

This innovative physician employment model will give employers a marketplace advantage over their competitors and help them win the physician recruitment and retention wars currently raging among employers.

This model, when packaged properly for an employer's physicians, can include:

1. Safe, legally compliant turnkey outsourcing through a comprehensive physician agency. The agency will manage things on the doctor's side and make sure none of it goes off the rails. *Some employers pay for all or part of this service due to the net benefit they receive from the physician's conversion to this model.

2. Larger household income for their employed doctors in this model after the doctor's fair market value compensation is routed through the optimal small business structures that lead to enhanced retained income. Their PC-employment lite doctors will keep more of their earnings in comparison to their traditionally employed doctors.

3. Their employed doctors will have Individualized benefit plans sourced for the doctor and paid for by the doctor's PC, allowing the employer to shed expenses ranging from $30,000 to $50,000 per doctor.

4. A built-in burnout prevention program helps doctors hold onto their personal and professional autonomy while remaining tightly aligned with their employer.

5. It is an innovative employment model that helps employers retain their most productive and valuable physician employees. This is because they can now reward their high-performing doctors via the conversion to a PC-employment lite model that includes the multiple physician benefits previously mentioned.

6. This is a systemic change to labor expenses that will save employers money on physician employment costs in an era where managing escalating staffing expenses is a common strategic need. As was previously noted, be aware that employment lite is a type of contracted labor but should be ideally categorized as a subtype of employment rather than being framed as a contracted service like a locum.

RETAIN-RETAIN

Ultimately, this is a physician retention program for big businesses that simultaneously allows the individual doctor to retain more income through their PC business model. The implementation of this simple systemic change benefits each stakeholder financially through the retention of their most valuable asset. It's like finding the holy grail of business strategies for both parties.

Owning your PC that can be used in connection with your professional services does not mean that the other half of your current employment contract will embrace it. The deployment of your

PC into the marketplace will lead you to encounter gatekeepers who will resist it due to their unfamiliarity with this novel version of your small business superpower.

But your decision to create a micro-PC as a small business envelope for your professional services does not depend on your gatekeeper's approval. The fact is that its formation is completely under your control. No one else can force you to do it or abandon it.

Choosing to create a PC early in your career will place you in the position to use it incrementally as opportunities arise and as employers come to embrace it. However, since it takes time and resources to create it, you don't want to wait to encounter an opportunity and then scramble to create it after the fact. Instead, you should begin by starting it now.

SUMMARY

- You will meet resistance to forming your PC and employment lite contract from many stakeholders, but the most important force that you will have overcome is yourself.

- PC-employment lite saves employers money while increasing the doctor's household income.

- PC-employment lite offers many advantages to employers and employees.

CHAPTER 11

HOW TO FORM YOUR PC

DO IT RIGHT

MANY OF YOU ARE FRUGAL DO-IT-YOURSELF EXPERTS. FUELED by your broad intelligence and the instant accessibility of "how to" videos and websites, there is a temptation to try to figure out most things on your own. I understand because I have a similar mindset. Before I outsource anything, I will usually take a cursory look on the web to see just how hard it is to do it myself. Over the years, this has worked out well sometimes—and other times not so well.

For example, about twenty years ago, when I started the previously mentioned marriage mentor organization, it had very little money. So I figured that as its thrifty founder, I could complete the 501c3 application and get it approved. You know, as doctors, we don't lack confidence. So six months later, and after a few IRS-directed revisions to the 250-page document, it was approved. Knowing what I know now, I would have never taken on such a huge endeavor and would have outsourced it to an agent that does this all the time.

And then there was the time that my wife and I set out to remodel the kitchen in our house that was built in 1870. It looked like a simple demolition process to remove a wall that would make the kitchen bigger. Unfortunately, when the wall came down, it revealed a critical supporting wall for the floor above it. Yikes! My home contractor friend just shook his head after arriving to assess the cause of my urgent call. Thankfully, he was able to fix my mistake without a disaster occurring. Sometimes you are better off having a professional do the job from the start!

When it comes to starting your PC, don't jump in via LegalZoom as an easy way to get your PC off the ground. Your PC should be organized under experienced legal guidance by someone who understands doctors so that it is designed to support your professional and individualized needs and goals. Much like every doctor is uniquely different from one another, so every PC is different from another. Both you and your individual business are colored by your interests, personalities, goals, and purposes, and that uniqueness is transmitted into the structure of your PC.

While any licensed doctor can start and form a PC, you should hire a professional to help you make sure it is done right rather than try to do it yourself.

WARNING

I am not a lawyer, and any of the following material should not be construed as legal advice to you.

Since you and I are both medical professionals and not business attorneys, many of the ins and outs of setting up and managing a professional medical corporation will likely not be familiar to you.

The following will walk you through some terminologies and introduce you to how PCs are established and governed. This will inform you about what to expect as you walk through this process with a professional.

TIMING

You may wonder when is the earliest that you could form a PC and start streaming your income through it. The short answer is that this can occur sometime after your first year of post-graduate training within your specialty.

The critical element for most states is that you must have an independent medical license.[75] Of note, this is different from your training certificate, which is a form of a license issued to physicians who are in an accredited residency program. This license permits you to practice under supervision with your training institute and can be used in that institution until you graduate. This type of licensure does not allow you to practice independently.

---

75 "Navigating State Medical Licensure," *AMA* (blog), American Medical Association, accessed November 27, 2022, https://www.ama-assn.org/medical-residents/transition-resident-attending/navigating-state-medical-licensure.

Determining when to seek a full independent medical license during your residency will depend on personal priorities and what your training institution supports. Some residents, for instance, may seek licensure to moonlight during their training years. In addition, some graduate medical education (GME) institutions may require that a physician be licensed at a certain point in their training.

Regarding the timing of your independent license, I believe doing it sooner rather than later offers you more professional flexibility. I obtained mine soon after my first post-graduate year so that I could moonlight. I saw moonlighting as a great way to make additional income.

More importantly, I believed it would benefit my professional development because it forced me to think and act independently. I do not doubt that I matured as a physician faster due to experiences like being the only doctor in a rural Virginia hospital during sixty-hour weekends in which I managed all inpatients and staffed the ER.

These intense moonlighting experiences ultimately allowed for the diverse use of my professional skills to earn more income but also opened the door to the possibility of starting my PC. I didn't start a PC then, but based on what I know now, I wish I had.

In thirty-three states, MDs can obtain a license to independently practice medicine after just one year of training, and in thirty-seven states, DOs can do the same. For most states, you will be required to pass Step 3 of the USMLE or COMLEX before applying.[76]

---

76 Carolyn Schierhorn, "Practicing after One Year of GME: Is It Feasible? Should It Be?," *The DO*, February 5, 2014, https://thedo.osteopathic.org/2014/02/practicing-after-one-year-of-gme-is-it-feasible-should-it-be/.

Thus, it is possible to form a PC after one year of post-graduate training if you believe it will benefit you with your side hustles. I recommend you check with your state on its rules regarding this. If your state allows for it, you can form a PC to funnel your moonlighting income through it. I suggest you work with your tax professional to set this up properly.

If you are an attending physician, it's never too late to create and use this special small business power you have earned. It applies to just about any job situation you are in or plan to be in. As I have demonstrated with my personal experience, even a mid-career physician can benefit from it. I recommend you do it now by following the steps I outline in the remainder of this chapter.

STEPS TO START A PC

The steps to forming a PC for medical professionals are very similar to starting a regular corporation such as an LLC. I will walk you through the process and highlight the important things to note for each step. I strongly recommend that you seek legal counsel and advice from a financial professional, such as an accountant, before starting this process.

1. Decide on a Name

In many states, you will be restricted to choosing the first or last name of one or more stockholders as the name; for example, "Tod A Stillson MD, PC." Some states will allow you to choose a fictitious name, but this usually requires some extra steps to file a permit with the state. No matter your route, you'll need to ensure your name is not already taken. Most states will have a way for you to do a preliminary business name search on the state website, most commonly under the secretary of state.

2. Appoint a Registered Agent

This can be a person or a company who will be the contact between your corporation and the government. They will file the necessary paperwork and receive official legal correspondence. This cannot be the corporation itself, but it can be a person affiliated with the company, like yourself. Your agent, attorney, or accountant will often fill this role. Check with your state on its corporate agent requirements.

3. File the Articles of Incorporation

The Articles of Incorporation are basically what formally start your corporation. They have to be filed with the state. This document will contain the corporation's name, address, and purpose, the Registered Agent's information, and the number of shares the corporation can issue. This document should specifically state that it is for a professional corporation.

4. Send in the Statement of Information or Business Entity Report

Each state will vary on the name of this component, calling it something like a statement of information, an annual report, or the business entity report. This will contain critical business information such as registered agent, officer(s), business address, mailing address, and email.

5. Register with Your State's Governing Medical Board

All of your shareholders must hold valid medical licenses to be part of the medical corporation. You must also register the company with your state's governing board. Each state has specific laws that govern the shareholders.

6. Draft Your Bylaws

Bylaws are internal governing documents for corporations, while an operating agreement lays out internal operating procedures for an LLC.

Since you are setting up a professional corporation, you will need to have bylaws, which are the rules and procedures by which your corporation operates. States can vary on whether the state oversight agency needs a copy of them. This document specifies who can be issued shares and who can and will serve as the board's executive officers as president, vice president, etc.

Although the shareholders must be licensed as a physician, this does not mean that the corporation cannot have employees who are not licensed practitioners, such as a spouse.

After legally forming your corporation, you'll need to hold a Board of Directors meeting and put your bylaws into effect. Because this is a critical element in setting up your corporation, you will want a trained professional to draft and oversee this document.

This is where working with someone with experience setting up PCs is very helpful. An experienced agent who understands you, your needs, and the best business structure to support your short- and long-term goals is even more valuable here. You can do this generically or in a highly individualized manner. You will pay more for it to be individualized with built-in business and tax advantages, and I can assure you that this extra work and expense will be worth it.

7. Registrations and Taxes

You will need to apply for an EIN (Employer ID Number) from the IRS, register with your state, pay corporate taxes to your state, obtain state business licenses and permits, and possibly apply for various other local licenses, depending on your city and county regulations. This is where an experienced business attorney can guide you through this process to ensure you don't miss anything.

You will want to decide on your tax designation as an S-Corp or C-Corp. Most doctors will choose an S-Corp status as it may help provide you with some business and tax advantages. As a reminder, S-Corp status will allow the corporate income to flow through to the shareholders and be taxed on their individual income tax level. This is called "pass-through" taxation and helps small businesses avoid being taxed excessively.

8. Open a Business Bank Account

Once you've filed the appropriate paperwork and established your corporate identity, you will need to open a business bank account. This ensures that you keep your business assets separate from personal expenses. You'll likely need your Articles of Incorporation, bylaws, and EIN to complete this step.

Costs to Start

Always remember that you get what you pay for, so I recommend that you don't try to form or maintain a PC—or patch the components together from multiple sources.

The costs are hard to measure due to the individual nature of a PC, the tax-advantaged plans built in, state-specific considerations associated with a PC, and the preferred tax designation.

So beginning with this information, the following are some cost comparisons from basic setups to progressively more personalized sources who can help you create your PC:

- Using an online company would keep your costs at around **$1,500-$2,500**.

- A community-based general lawyer will charge you **$3,000-$5,000** to set things up relatively simplistically.

- An experienced physician-centric lawyer will charge you around **$5,000-$10,000** to do all of the steps involved with some specificity to your specialty along with some built-in fringe benefits and months of wrap-around legal advice that will make the return on investment worth the extra costs.

- An experienced lawyer who comprehensively understands you, your goals, your needs, and the best way to formulate a PC structure to benefit your long-term plan will charge you between **$10,000** and **$15,000** to set things up in compliance with your state and with a highly personalized fringe benefit package and extended wrap-around legal advice built into it. This piece will save you sufficient money to easily pay for this extra expense, making it worthwhile due to its business and personal benefits.

STEPS TO MAINTAINING A PC

You'll also need to follow local regulations to maintain your PC. Each state has different requirements on PC reporting and tax filing, so make sure you understand what is expected where you live. Enclosed is a summary of the required steps involved with maintaining your small business. Many owners choose a registered agent to provide these services for them.

1. State Report

Most states will require an annual or biennial report to the state to update business information such as registered agent, officer(s), business address, mailing address, and email.

2. Taxes

- File annual federal and state income taxes

- Pay federal, state, and local taxes for any employees via estimated quarterly withholding

- Register to pay state unemployment insurance taxes

- Provide annual W-2 earnings statements to any employee

- Provide annual K-1 statements to shareholders

3. Annual Board of Directors Meeting and Minutes

Most states require you to record annual shareholder and board of director meeting minutes. Important items to include in this document are the meeting's date, time, location, who wrote the minutes, the names of the members in attendance, a brief description of the meeting agenda, details about what the members discussed, decisions made, voting actions taken, and election of officers. Typically your agent or attorney can help provide these minutes for you and record them for you.

You'll note these steps associated with maintaining your PC include a mixture of both legal and accounting components. Thus having an accountant and lawyer who work well together is really helpful; a comprehensive team is even better.

It is also worth noting that keeping accounting books, payroll, bank management, and other business functions are not mandated by the state or federal authorities but are fundamental to the smooth operation of any small business. The most common model that I see for supporting this is employing a spouse to book-keep and manage these items. Employing your spouse through your PC unlocks numerous benefits for your household, such as the ability to open retirement plans for both you and your spouse. Alternatively, these functions can be outsourced to your accountant as well.

Costs to Maintain

In maintaining your PC, you will typically want to engage a lawyer and an accounting professional due to the steps connected with maintaining your small business.

Depending on the scope of your PC's business activity, your annual legal, accounting, and tax management fees could **range from $500 to $25,000** annually. If you do most of the work yourself through online services like QuickBooks and Turbo-Tax, you can maintain a modest PC for a small amount of money annually.

I know that is a wide range, but the size of your PC's business activities can vary widely from person to person, and its complexities and the scope of services from an accountant will determine the exact cost.

For example, if you use your PC through your primary job in an employment lite agreement, the cost will be higher. On the other hand, if you use your PC solely to flow side income, there will be less business activity. Extreme do-it-your-selfers can save lots of money through self-management by using self-guided online services for bookkeeping, business activity, banking, and taxes. Again, I would be cautious about this, but if you are doing this in baby steps, you probably can do it yourself at the beginning.

As you can see, choosing to start a PC and then maintaining it will cost you a good sum of money. However, it will easily pay for itself financially as well as holistically make your life better.

Remember that these business expenses are deductible from your corporate operations and thus can and should be viewed differently than a consumer purchase that comes from your household expenses. For example, purchasing a car for $25,000 is an income-losing, depreciating asset deducted from your household funds. However, a PC is an income-producing, income-retaining, and appreciating asset that is purchased by your own business and takes no money from your household funds.

OPERATING YOUR BUSINESS

I understand you have little exposure and training to operate a small business. Thus the financial terms and steps associated with bookkeeping and accounting can feel a little overwhelming. Just like our medical training is like learning a foreign language, when you begin to run your own business, you will have to become more familiar with the foreign language of business and accounting. I recommend that you work with a trusted accounting and tax professional on all the components of bookkeeping, accounting, and taxes.

One option is to employ your spouse or significant other as your corporate bookkeeper. That is what I do. Beyond sharing the workload, this can unify you in the joining operation of the small business as well as unlock numerous financial benefits to your household. Every household's situation is different regarding how this works best, so it does have to be individualized to your specific household. However, if your spouse or significant other also has a career, you will need to work with your accounting services professional to sort out what will work best for you in regard to your bookkeeping, accounting, and tax workflow.

Outsource to an Agency

When I started a PC and converted to an employment lite agreement, the one-year return on investment for my business expenses was well over 350 percent. Although results can vary, this can certainly help you decide to do the same thing if you are in a similar position.

The one-year return on investment will be much less if your primary job does not flow through your PC. As previously stated, $40,000 or more in side income is usually the tipping point to make it cost-effective for your side work. This can vary based on your individual income and your overall household income.

However, assuming it is cost-effective for your particular professional life, I recommend you consider outsourcing this entire process to a team of professionals who will do this work on your behalf. You can save money doing all of this yourself, but the nuances can be a little challenging if you lack small business experience. In many regards outsourcing it to a team of professionals is like hitting the "easy" button, as they ensure it is done properly and make it all turnkey.

The best agencies can provide comprehensive legal, accounting, and business services under one roof, but not every agency will understand all of the nuances of PC-employment lite agreements and the associated optimal business wrap-around for them.

When you take into consideration the business coaching, investing, accounting, tax, and legal services all fully integrated into the package for a complete PC-employment lite model, you could be looking at $25,000 to $35,000 for the comprehensive business setup. You can plan for a 20-30 percent smaller total for the annual maintenance of the complete program. Again for this price, the scope of services provided for your small business will be cost-effective, comprehensive, and turnkey.

A qualified agency will typically provide a full feasibility evaluation before making this conversion to confirm that forming a PC will benefit your household financially. Ideally, they will do it via a side-by-side view that compares a "what if" version contrasting you without a PC vs. with a PC (and its tax-efficient business structures). They will also provide a full scope of services documenting and outlining how they will support the setup and operation of your small business.

When you form a PC, you will have many options for creating your business, but enlisting help from others will be your best move.

SUMMARY

- There are multiple steps associated with starting and maintaining a PC.

- The best micro-PC is individually built to support your unique life.

- You should work with experienced professionals to help you form your PC.

- PCs are not cheap, but they easily pay for themselves.

- You can start your PC after you are individually licensed in your state.

CHAPTER 12

YOU NEED YOUR OWN TEAM

AGENTS AND OPTIONS

DOCTORS ARE A LOT LIKE PROFESSIONAL ATHLETES. YOU ARE both an individual and a small business that generates downstream income for larger corporations that want to use your professional services and influence.

This is why you are seeing progressive changes in the athletic and entertainment marketplace that allow collegiate and professional athletes to monetize the power of their name, image, or likeness (NIL). Previously these assets were exploited for the profits of big corporations. This space represented the downstream revenue associated with the contracted athlete beyond the professional services on the playing field.

For college athletes, that contract is for an educational scholarship; for professionals, it is monetary compensation. Unlike college athletes, professionals are also allowed to form side gig endorsement agreements as long as they don't compete with their employer's professional services.

A classic example for athletes is shoe sponsorship. You should note here that, much like an athlete, your monetized life as a doctor is much larger than the professional service you provide to your employer's playing field. You have a small business superpower that allows you to monetize your professional skills in multiple spaces beyond a single employer.

Although you are not "drafted" like athletes, you are essentially a "free agent" who is free to move from employer to employer as you sign term-limited professional services contracts with companies who are interested in your clinical services.

For employers, the physician "draft" pools are the resident graduates each year, and the "free agent" pools are the physician recruitment companies that attract available physicians and pair them with employers. These recruiters are paid by prospective employers, which means their alignment is biased and incentivized to benefit employers and not doctors.

As you know, each professional athlete is allowed to voluntarily choose an agent who represents their personal and professional matters, including their contractual relationships with their employer, union, and personal interests. This agent negotiates contractual terms related to their client's services with a prospective employer through a professional services contract. Salary, bonuses, and renegotiation terms are diverse, and the athlete's union ensures the core is relatively standardized.

With the help of their agent, many athletes organize themselves corporately for business and tax purposes so that their primary income (professional services) is wisely organized with their passive income/side hustles (endorsements and appearances). By surrounding themselves with a wise agency, professional athletes optimize their high-income cash flow, enhance their marketplace value (free agency), and prepare themselves for retirement. For the same reasons, you, as a physician, need an agent.

Although the federal government does not allow for the unionization of doctors, they do allow for agency and legal representation. But for some reason, doctors overwhelmingly ignore this option and trust their wisdom in connection with the goodwill of their employer's legal department to organize their professional contracts. This is a mistake.

Every high-income earning profession is represented by an agent, union, or both. This is common to entertainers, athletes, and many who offer professional services, such as teachers and engineers. Physicians are the outliers in this process. Beyond the financial benefits of hiring an agency to represent you, an agency will help you organize your personal and professional life so that it favorably meets your goals.

YOU NEED AN AGENT

The real problem begins when you passively give your employer full control of your employment agreement or professional services. In so doing, you let them fully organize the terms and the structure, including its impact on your personal and professional life.

They will lead you to believe that it is safest to give up your small business and professional services to them in order to remain compliant with federal and state regulations. They logically reason that this is the only way they can guarantee your 100 percent compliance with all the federal and state laws that govern healthcare services for physicians.

In this context, they assume you don't have a legal team to ensure that you and your small business will comply with all professional services and business laws. If you hire an agent, you will now have someone to help you with all of this.

Most doctors just don't know about the business of engaging in contracts with big corporations. However, the truth is that you have control over it if you are willing to hire an agent to represent you, thus unlocking all the possibilities based on your individual needs and preferences.

I want to pause here and distinguish that hiring an agent is not the same as hiring a contract review agency. Although these companies are important, all they will do is make sure that your traditional employment contract is fairly organized for you. It is a one-and-done relationship.

In contrast, an agent is an ongoing professional relationship in which the agency uses all of its resources to ensure that your professional and personal life is maximized via the professional services contract that you have with your primary employer, but also includes a more comprehensive structure that supports every facet of your business, professional, and personal life.

I met Ben when I was being coached to move towards an employment lite agreement by my business consultants. His father was a pathologist, and thus, Ben understood the business needs of physicians and their families. Trained as a tax attorney, he has a keen eye for business structures and their impact on a doctor's home.

He immediately set me at ease as he gathered personal information about me, my family, and my professional goals. In the end, he listened closely and formed my corporate bylaws that were fully wrapped around my individual household needs and maximized my financial bottom line.

Ben is the kind of person you need on your side, and he would ideally be someone who was part of your comprehensive team.

An agent and their business team can help build the right professional business model and negotiate the terms of an employment agreement within that business model that will still be a win-win for both parties. It just takes a bit of proactive assertiveness to hire an agent and their business team to help represent your interests in this equation. They can help you form your PC and explore whether a PC-employment lite agreement makes sense for you now or even later.

AFTER RECRUITMENT OPTIONS

Much like athletes, the recruitment process between you and your employer is filled with promises and trust-building. It is a courtship that involves identifying whether you are suitable partners for the future. But this initial matching primarily involves the psycho-social elements and a clear path to your professional preferences. Once these boxes are checked for both parties, and the corporate recruitment team has landed its prize (you) with all the associated promises, they will lateral things to the business-legal office to close the deal.

Make sure to patiently organize and document all of the corporate promises made during the recruitment process. Too often, these promises are not documented in the contract as memorandums of understanding and are just understood by people in the chain of command. You will soon discover that the memory of those promises disappears quickly due to the rapid turnover of administrators in medicine. Wisely, your employer's legal department purposefully ignores those promises made to you and prefers to focus on "boilerplate contracts" that are "cleaner" due to their equality for all physician employees in the organization.

Remember that although your employer may be benevolent and trustworthy, their alignment is with their board of directors, not you. Those same administrators earn corporate performance bonuses for the financial bottom line of their organization. The lower your compensation package, the more your employer will profit from you. Additionally, the fewer "promises" documented in the contract, the better. Getting you signed is the goal, and leaving the promises in the realm of 1:1 relationships is preferred.

This is a great time to tap into the power of your unified professional team through an agency rather than a series of professional silos that you have to unify on your own.

THE POWER OF A COLLABORATIVE TEAM

The Mayo Clinic in Rochester, Minnesota, began 150 years ago as the medical practice of Dr. Worrell Mayo and his two sons,

William and Charles. By developing a team approach to specialized care and an integrated medical record, the Mayo Clinic developed into one of the largest group practices in the world, known for treating specialized problems and delivering complex, multi-specialty care. One of the keys to the success of the Mayo Clinic has been the ability of members of the staff to collaborate together face to face in real-time to address the patient's needs and conditions. The efficiency gained from shared knowledge, professional interaction, and a unified plan of care makes this a compelling model of care.

A similar collaborative model of professionals is needed for doctors whose personal and professional needs often fuse together due to their integrated nature. Even though most of you recognize this multidisciplinary case conference is beneficial in your medical world, you will fail to recognize your need for it in your personal world.

SELF-SUFFICIENT

High performers like you tend to prefer working alone. You are highly intelligent, confident, and relatively self-sufficient and, therefore, are likely to opt for some form of self-management in your professional life. The problem is that most are ill-equipped to do this themselves. You are conditioned not to ask for help; thus, this approach often leads to a non-unified, poorly organized system of silos that surrounds your personal and professional life.

I recognize that doctors will typically break into three basic groups when it comes to managing business, time, and money in their life:

1. **10 percent actively manage it themselves.** These are the White Coat Investor Network followers who enjoy the time investment in self-discovery and self-management of these areas.

2. **15 percent actively manage it through a blend of DIY and outsourcing.** This includes hiring a financial planner, lawyer, accountant, personal assistant, nanny, or others to off-load the non-work obligations and tasks.

3. **75 percent passively manage.** This represents the majority who complacently let the chips fall in place. They trust the people who vie for their attention and business as they recognize their time constraints along with their high income. Their support team is typically built haphazardly and at a higher cost due to the tyranny of the urgent.

For most, the best move is to surround yourself with a trusted team of professionals who will help you thrive holistically. Ultimately, a life coached by others will surpass the self-sufficient life.

One of the critical infrastructure elements that you should create is a professional team that advises and supports your life journey.

The result of not creating your team will be the formation of a group of professional silos that surround you.

SILOS AND PASSIVELY CREATED TEAMS

This disjointed group of silos will slowly crop up as you progress through the stages of your career. It is usually an additive process driven by your felt need at the time. For example, you ask an attorney for legal guidance only when a matter arises; you ask an accountant to advise on your taxes once a year as you meet to file them; you meet with a financial planner when you are unsure how to invest your money. Each of these professionals will interface with you in silos that are blinded from one another. Their episodic professional care is executed based on the need of the moment.

In this à la carte model, your life is scabbed together in a haphazard architecture that is based upon the needs that are visible to you at the time. It often lacks a holistic direction and often forces you to be a mediator between competing recommendations from each professional silo. Although they all work on your behalf, they don't communicate or operate as a team moving you in the same direction by following unified goals.

It's like only using the ER and specialist for your medical care rather than using your PCP. Acute care through the ER rarely considers the holistic components of chronic disease and wellness. Likewise, specialists who manage your chronic disease in a vacuum are often oblivious to your other acute, chronic illness, and wellness needs. But a PCP will holistically manage all three elements together in collaboration with the specialty care and acute medical needs.

I can't tell you how often a patient comes to me confused about what to do with competing medical advice from various specialists, and I am left to help mediate the best course of action as I collaborate with the patient.

Again, this is a similar tension you may feel when your attorney, accountant, and financial planner communicate competing advice to you. Each is correct in their professional counsel given to you in a silo, but you are left with the difficult choice of which person to follow.

This is the outcome associated with a passive approach to building your team. It ends up being built in an asynchronous pattern filled with professionals who are not working together but are working independently based upon your self-identified needs.

DOCTORS BENEFIT FROM TEAMS

When you are placed in a position to deploy your strengths as a decision-maker on a team, you will typically flourish both personally and professionally. This is another one of the secret sauces associated with living your best life.

I learned from my near burnout experience that building teams around me to support my personal and professional life resulted in a greater sense of satisfaction due to the way it amplified my decision-making strengths and allowed my team members to use their strengths.

When you create a physician-centric team, you invite others to help you holistically address the visible and invisible threats to your autonomy. Thus, they must understand doctors and the unique pressures associated with physician employment. This is why physician-focused agencies are critical to use as you form your professional team.

BUILDING A TEAM FOR PERSONAL SUPPORT

Doctors and their families live complicated lifestyles that seem to always be time-crunched. To meet the long list of competing time demands, you will have to be willing to outsource elements of your personal life. You just can't do it all.

This concept of outsourcing and teamwork goes far beyond your professional world. Face it: there are a lot of menial tasks and activities associated with doing life outside of medicine. This personal scut work is one of the many components that compete for our most valuable daily resource—time.

I want to refer you back to the four-burner theory again. Even after your training is complete, medicine will consume as much of your attention as you allow it to. You must be careful not to let it become all-consuming and burn out the flames that bring balance and a deep sense of well-being to your life.

OFF-LOAD TO GAIN TIME

As an attending, you will become progressively focused on your family and personal life outside medicine. It is the inevitable outcome as your life grows. This is often the zone in which many of you will decide to start your family. Adding family members will inevitably require more of your time and the need for multi-tasking. Striking a work-life balance is a dance that will be managed for the rest of your professional career. I encourage you to outsource non-essential time stealers in your life so you can maximally enjoy both your professional and personal life.

The more you can outsource and minimize time stealers like chores, commuting, and things you don't enjoy doing, the better off you will be. The only exception to this minimization process is sleeping and nutrition, which you should not sacrifice or neglect due to their profound effect on your well-being. Cutting out your personal and professional time commitments is a highly individualized decision tree, but work will be the dominant force during your waking hours, and you have to be careful not to let it consume you at the expense of your personal time.

GIVE UP MONEY TO GAIN TIME

Ashley Whillans, a Harvard professor, has done significant research on over 100,000 working people worldwide. Her studies have found, in her own words, that:

> *"People who are willing to give up money to gain more free time—by, say, working fewer hours or paying to outsource disliked tasks—experience more fulfilling social relationships, more satisfying careers, and more joy, and overall, live happier lives."*

This important illuminating truth about life, tasks, time, and money will repeatedly play out in your professional and personal life. There is a tension between how you spend your time and money that you must consider as you seek to live your best life. As a physician, you have two primary options for finding the sweet spot in the tension between time and money.

1. Cut back your work time demands to a threshold that provides you the desired life balance, and then be content with making less money in exchange for this.

This may force you to live a more modest lifestyle and delay reaching financial independence. You will value present balance and satisfaction at this end of the spectrum.

2. Work your job at whatever time is necessary to support your desired income level, but simultaneously minimize and outsource all other obligations and tasks. This could provide you with an elevated lifestyle or an earlier arrival at financial independence. But rarely both. You value the present lifestyle and future independence on this end of the spectrum.

TIME STEALERS AND OUTSOURCING

In your personal life, a host of tasks are associated with operating a busy household and living a robust lifestyle. I encourage you to create support teams around you to help complete these tasks. This tapestry of off-loading tedious tasks will relieve their burden on you and provide you with extra time for things more important to you.

You do have a lot of options to outsource these time-stealers. This is personal and partner-driven, but I encourage you to filter this through a return on investment model that includes finances and time as the key component. As you evaluate which elements you want to manage and which elements you want to outsource, focus on gaining net personal time because it will positively affect your well-being.

There are numerous components to this outsourcing puzzle, so let me try to organize it in a spreadsheet format:

Outsourcing Options for Physicians

	Source rather than DIY	ROI Dollars	ROI Personal Time	Comments
Work-Professional Employment-Contract	Agent, lawyer, contract review company	++++	++++	Recommend fee only for a service provider. Due to most physician's **business literacy**, this is worth every dollar with a high ROI.
Personal Finance, Investment & Debt Management	Financial planner, bank, financial company	++++	++++	Recommend fee only for a service provider. Due to most physician's **financial literacy**, this is worth every dollar with a high ROI.
Taxes	Accountant, tax preparation company (in-person or virtual)	+++	+	Multiple strategies are involved depending on your taxable entities. Large $$$ in retained income for tax-wise through a small business structure.
Business & Side Business	Lawyer, agent, investors, salesman	++++	++	Active vs. passive involvement is your key decision, especially in real estate. Employment Lite through a PC has an over 300% ROI.
Banking	Banker, accountant	+	+++	This is more of an issue of convenience and accessibility, but certain banking services can be beneficial and save time.
Housing	Property manager, realtor	++	+++	Rent, condo, or full home ownership. Many pitfalls and considerations here, especially if you buy a doctor's house too early.
House Maintenance	Landscaper, mower, snow removal, irrigation, pool care, HVAC, plumber, electrician	+	++++	Typically worth every dollar
Housekeeping	Housekeeper/maid	+	++++	Typically worth every dollar
Meals	Personal chef, online services, eating out	+++	++++	Highly variable based on personal preferences of food sources, is not budget-friendly vs. DIY, but is very time-friendly in regards to ROI.
Shopping/Groceries	House manager, online services	+	++++	Easy place to gain time in exchange for money.
Childcare	Daycare, nanny	++	++++	Can vary based on dual career families vs. stay-at-home partners
Commuting/Transportation	Public vs. private transportation	++++	++++	Geographic arbitrage connected to work-home-leisure movement patterns. Multiple pitfalls for doctors here.
Vacations	Vacation planners	++	++	You choose the location and time frame, others plan the details for you.

Figure 12.2

Figure 12.2 is not meant to be comprehensive since there are multiple individual considerations regarding personal outsourcing. But as you can see, four areas stick out as having large upsides for your dollars and time. They include:

1. Work-Professional Employment Contract

2. Personal Finances-Investment-Debt Management

3. Housing

4. Commuting-Transportation

Each of these areas is worthy of serious consideration for outsourcing as you assemble a team of people around you that can help solve your time pressures.

When you can surround yourself with others that help you maximize your personal and professional time, you will have invested in what most consider your most important earned asset—time.

TIME IS MOST IMPORTANT

One of the outcomes of forming your PC along with an employment lite agreement is that it provides you with more self-directed time. Instead of spending time chasing additional sources of income that help you reach your net worth goals, a PC allows you to RETAIN and SAVE more of your money in a tax-friendly manner that greatly accelerates your net worth while you work the same amount. Thus you can spend less time working and more time in Stage 3 of your career.

In the end, PC-employment lite is a very time-efficient method for increasing your household income. But let me remind you that more money will not lead to more happiness, but having more time is associated with greater happiness. Some additional thoughts to ponder in regard to how time is more valuable than money include:

- You can't make more time, but you can always make more money.

- A day off is worth more than a day's pay.

- Time allows for more experiences.

- Experiences lead to longer-lasting happiness than material possessions due to their connection with lasting memories and positive relationships.

- At the end of our lives, we never want more money, but we often want more time.

- Money is the means for buying you autonomous time, and control over your time will enhance your well-being.

Much like wisely using your earned assets to form a PC will allow you to retain a portion of your earned income, so wisely using your assets to create support teams will allow you to retain more of your most important asset—time.

As you traverse through your professional life, allowing others to help you proactively manage your assets will support your holistic well-being and allow you to live your best life as a doctor.

SUMMARY

- You need an agent.

- You need a professional support team.

- Outsource liberally because your time is your most valuable asset.

- Take days off work to use your time for experiences with those who matter most to you.

CONCLUSION

THE ROAD LESS TRAVELED

OVER 100 YEARS AGO, ROBERT FROST DESCRIBED THE COGNITIVE challenge of choosing a less-traveled path in his 1915 poem "The Road Not Taken." In the poem, Frost identified two seemingly similar paths or roads. Then, after a careful review of each road, the individual represented in the poem opted to follow the less traveled road, as noted by the words of the last stanza:

> *Two roads diverged in a wood, and I—*
>
> *I took the one less traveled by,*
>
> *And that has made all the difference.*

When I became aware of a better employment path and began to journey down the less-traveled road, it made all the difference for my professional life to thrive.

Sadly, you are likely to miss out on your best life because this less-traveled path is nearly completely hidden from your view, and it's certainly not the path that is being followed by the majority of your peers.

Your conditioning associated with becoming a practicing doctor creates a blind spot to the entry point to this route. The real problem is that you are unaware of the possibilities for your best life because you will indiscriminately trust your peers and employer to define it for you. It turns out, paradoxically, your best life is within the same employer's harbor as your traditional job, but your best move is to activate your small business powers and start a PC within that harbor. This will restore your professional autonomy and improve your financial well-being.

This best life is likely to evade if you lack the vision and the will to rethink anything beyond what your employer and peers have convinced you are the best version of a doctor's good life. You don't have to accept good when it can be great. A good life is secured when you choose traditional employment, but your best life will be experienced when you form your PC and use it with an employment lite agreement.

This book has provided you with the tools, guidance, and inspiration to help you choose a less-traveled road leading to a much better personal and professional life.

The evidence points towards the need for an innovative change to the physician employment system that includes rethinking how you can use your assets, especially your small business superpower. This will provide a minimally disruptive systemic solution to the growing physician burnout crisis.

Using all your earned assets to self-define your personal and professional world will lead to your best life. The zone of life between the plateaus of finishing your training and reaching financial independence is so dynamic that change and adaptation are normal and should be expected. By creating a flexible infrastructure that includes the formation of your small business PC, you will unlock many adaptive tools that will help you manage those changes best.

START, CHANGE, CHOOSE

I truly want to help you avoid the same mistakes I made in the first fifteen years of my career that nearly led me to burnout. I ended up in that crisis because I failed to recognize my need to start, change, and choose professional adaptations that would preserve my autonomy. So let me recount those steps that I believe every physician would benefit from to help them thrive in the modern system of healthcare:

1. **Start** your PC and use it with a progressive employment model like employment lite. This will restore your autonomy and small business superpower.

2. **Change** your self-sufficient tendencies and hire a physician-centric agency to help you reach your professional and personal goals and, thus, live your best life.

3. **Choose** to create a proactive plan that will help you avoid burnout as you prioritize your well-being.

These critical steps outlined above will support you in reaching your best life as a doctor while helping you avoid burnout. Choosing to do any of the three steps will help you, but the results of doing all three together will supersede the individual results.

START YOUR PC NOW

Your most important action step in response to reading this book is to start your PC, especially if you are at the beginning of your professional life.

I recommend that all licensed physicians do this because it represents one of the most important earned assets of your investment in your professional identity. In addition, starting your PC will help you preserve your professional autonomy.

Like finding a hidden treasure, my discovery of combining employment with a PC brought me back from the edge of burnout. It provided me with a hitherto secret employment structure of PC-employment lite that has re-inspired my career as an employed physician. Now I am flourishing, and I want you to do the same by following a similar path.

In reality, the COMBINATION of forming your PC while entering the employment space will prove to be the most powerful choice you can make to enjoy the best doctor's life that you have dreamed about.

In the end, it is indeed the road less traveled,

that has made all the difference,

for me.

FINAL THOUGHT

Systemic changes to the physician employment system are needed, and the PC-employment lite model non-disruptively fills this need. The next generation of doctors has the power to set in motion this movement by forming their PC before their first attending job and then assertively expecting their employers to support its use in the contract for their professional services.

I believe sharing the principles I've picked up over the years as an employed doctor can help address unrecognized knowledge gaps in your personal and professional life. This book is not comprehensive, so make sure to connect with professionals who understand doctors for more guidance or info in each area.

The ultimate power of this proposed systemic change involves much more than a simple contract structure. Rather it is an invigorated mindset that harkens back to the ethical and historical business origins that are foundational to our profession. You are indeed a small business that values the importance of preserving your professional autonomy while you proactively address your holistic well-being.

In the end, the PC-employment lite model provides a systemic solution that can help reduce the burnout crisis and restore your enthusiasm for delivering patient care.

Regardless of the road you choose, I hope you thrive in the world's greatest profession.

ACKNOWLEDGMENTS

I THANK MY COACH AND FIRST EDITOR, AMANDA WITT, WHO spent many hours reviewing this book. You have provided wonderful insights that significantly improved the final manuscript. Your personal reflections that grow out of being married to a young physician and your professional expertise as a marketing expert have been invaluable.

I am grateful to my friends at SimpliMD, who added their legal and business insights into how to best craft this book to fulfill its ultimate purpose of helping to improve young doctors' lives. Ben and Jeff, thank you!

Lastly, I want to thank my son, John, and my son-in-law, Garrick, who have thoughtfully trudged through each version of this manuscript. Their perspectives as a Generation Z medical resident (John) and young business professional (Garrick) have dramatically improved each manuscript copy.

ABOUT THE AUTHOR

 TOD STILLSON, MD, is a practicing family doctor in the Midwest who loves his job. He operates his PC through an employment lite agreement with his local hospital. You can follow him at www.doctorincorporated.com and subscribe to his regular blog posts. You can also join his physician community on Facebook at "Every Doctor Is A Business." If you need a professional agent, assistance in creating your PC, or help with comprehensively organizing a PC-employment lite agreement, contact him at SimpliMD.

Made in the USA
Monee, IL
30 March 2023